Teen
Alcoholism

Teen
Alcoholism

OTHER BOOKS OF RELATED INTEREST

Teen
Alcoholism

Laura K. Egendorf, *Book Editor*

Bonnie Szumski, *Editorial Director*
Scott Barbour, *Managing Editor*
Brenda Stalcup, *Series Editor*

Contemporary Issues
Companion

Greenhaven Press, Inc., San Diego, CA

Every effort has been made to trace the owners of copyrighted material. The articles in this volume may have been edited for content, length, and/or reading level. The titles have been changed to enhance the editorial purpose. Those interested in locating the original source will find the complete citation on the first page of each article.

No part of this book may be reproduced or used in any form or by any means, electrical, mechanical, or otherwise, including, but not limited to, photocopy, recording, or any information storage and retrieval system, without prior written permission from the publisher.

Library of Congress Cataloging-in-Publication Data

Teen alcoholism / Laura K. Egendorf, book editor.
    p.   cm. — (Contemporary issues companion)
   Includes bibliographical references and index.
   ISBN 0-7377-0682-1 (pbk. : alk. paper) —
ISBN 0-7377-0683-X (lib. : alk. paper)
   1. Teenagers—Alcohol use—United States. Alcoholism—United States. I. Egendorf, Laura K., 1973–   II. Series.

HV5135 .T44 2001
362.292'0835—dc21   00-068181
                                            CIP

CONTENTS

FOREWORD

In the news, on the streets, and in neighborhoods, individuals are confronted with a variety of social problems. Such problems may affect people directly: A young woman may struggle with depression, suspect a friend of having bulimia, or watch a loved one battle cancer. And even the issues that do not directly affect her private life—such as religious cults, domestic violence, or legalized gambling—still impact the larger society in which she lives. Discovering and analyzing the complexities of issues that encompass communal and societal realms as well as the world of personal experience is a valuable educational goal in the modern world.

Effectively addressing social problems requires familiarity with a constantly changing stream of data. Becoming well informed about today's controversies is an intricate process that often involves reading myriad primary and secondary sources, analyzing political debates, weighing various experts' opinions—even listening to firsthand accounts of those directly affected by the issue. For students and general observers, this can be a daunting task because of the sheer volume of information available in books, periodicals, on the evening news, and on the Internet. Researching the consequences of legalized gambling, for example, might entail sifting through congressional testimony on gambling's societal effects, examining private studies on Indian gaming, perusing numerous websites devoted to Internet betting, and reading essays written by lottery winners as well as interviews with recovering compulsive gamblers. Obtaining valuable information can be time-consuming—since it often requires researchers to pore over numerous documents and commentaries before discovering a source relevant to their particular investigation.

Greenhaven's Contemporary Issues Companion series seeks to assist this process of research by providing readers with useful and pertinent information about today's complex issues. Each volume in this anthology series focuses on a topic of current interest, presenting informative and thought-provoking selections written from a wide variety of viewpoints. The readings selected by the editors include such diverse sources as personal accounts and case studies, pertinent factual and statistical articles, and relevant commentaries and overviews. This diversity of sources and views, found in every Contemporary Issues Companion, offers readers a broad perspective in one convenient volume.

In addition, each title in the Contemporary Issues Companion series is designed especially for young adults. The selections included in every volume are chosen for their accessibility and are expertly edited in consideration of both the reading and comprehension levels of the audience. The structure of the anthologies also enhances accessibility. An introductory essay places each issue in context and provides helpful facts such as historical background or current statistics and legislation that pertain to the topic. The chapters that follow organize the material and focus on specific aspects of the book's topic. Every essay is introduced by a brief summary of its main points and biographical information about the author. These summaries aid in comprehension and can also serve to direct readers to material of immediate interest and need. Finally, a comprehensive index allows readers to efficiently scan and locate content.

The Contemporary Issues Companion series is an ideal launching point for research on a particular topic. Each anthology in the series is composed of readings taken from an extensive gamut of resources, including periodicals, newspapers, books, government documents, the publications of private and public organizations, and Internet websites. In these volumes, readers will find factual support suitable for use in reports, debates, speeches, and research papers. The anthologies also facilitate further research, featuring a book and periodical bibliography and a list of organizations to contact for additional information.

A perfect resource for both students and the general reader, Greenhaven's Contemporary Issues Companion series is sure to be a valued source of current, readable information on social problems that interest young adults. It is the editors' hope that readers will find the Contemporary Issues Companion series useful as a starting point to formulate their own opinions about and answers to the complex issues of the present day.

INTRODUCTION

Despite the fact that teenagers cannot drink legally in the United States, alcoholism and alcohol abuse are problems for many adolescents. A "Monitoring the Future Study" that was released in December 1999 by the National Institute on Drug Abuse and the University of Michigan's Institute for Social Research revealed that 53.2 percent of twelfth-grade students reported being drunk during the past year, with 30.8 percent having consumed five or more drinks in a row in the previous two weeks. Even eighth graders acknowledged some level of alcohol consumption; 18.5 percent reported having been drunk during the previous year. These younger drinkers are of particular concern to many people because youth who begin drinking before they are fifteen years old are four times more likely to develop a dependence on alcohol, compared to those who wait until they are of legal age. However, while it may seem that teenage alcoholism is a serious problem, there is disagreement as to what causes teen alcoholism and what steps can be taken to reduce it. Some people assert that the problem of teenage alcoholism is unique to America because its culture discourages underage drinking, as opposed to nations such as France, in which adolescents commonly drink wine with dinner. According to these researchers, the United States needs to change its attitude toward underage drinking so teenagers can learn responsible alcohol consumption. Other observers counter that the United States should continue to restrict teenagers' access to alcohol, arguing that encouraging consumption could exacerbate the problem.

In fact, the United States did not have a minimum legal drinking age for most of its history. After Prohibition was repealed in 1933, most states set a minimum age of twenty-one. That age was largely lowered to eighteen in the 1970s, when the voting age was also lowered. In the 1980s, due to the rash of teenagers dying in alcohol-related car crashes, states began to return to the age-21 standard.

In contrast to the United States, teenage drinking is legal in many countries. For example, Portugal and Belgium place no age restrictions on the purchase or consumption of alcohol. Austria, Great Britain, and Switzerland allow adolescents as young as sixteen to purchase alcohol and drink in public, although sometimes under certain restrictions (such as requiring that a parent be present if the teen wishes to drink). Depending on the province, the legal drinking age in Canada is eighteen or nineteen. According to Stanton Peele, a consultant for the International Center for Alcohol Policies in Washington, D.C., and the Wine Institute in San Francisco, such laws have the effect of minimizing teenage alcoholism. In an article in *Psychology Today*, he writes: "These countries believe that kids allowed to drink with their families become socialized to drinking moderately." David Hanson, a sociology professor at the State University of New York in Potsdam, offers an explanation as to why certain cultures and religions, in particular Mediterranean countries and Judaism, have lower levels of drinking problems. According to Hanson, people in these settings learn that abstaining from alcohol and drinking responsibly and in moderation are equally acceptable and "learn how to drink from an early age within the safe and supporting environment of the home." As it turns out, while less than one-tenth of the Jewish-American and Italian-American populations abstain from alcohol—compared to one-third of the general population—very few of the ninety-plus percent who drink have serious alcohol problems. A 1980 study of Jews living in an upstate New York community, conducted by Barry Glassner and Bruce Berg, found that only 0.1 percent could be defined as alcohol abusers.

Consequently, Peele, Hanson, and others maintain that the United States needs to loosen the restrictions it places on teenage drinkers. One suggestion is that parents should allow their children to drink at home, preferably at mealtime and under supervision. Learning to drink in this manner is safer, argue some researchers, because parents are more likely to ensure that their teenagers will not drink to excess and because they can show how moderate drinking—for example, a glass or two of wine with dinner—differs from binges at parties. Ruth Engs, a professor at Indiana University who has written extensively on alcohol, has suggested that the drinking age be lowered to 18 or 19 for consumption in environments such as school functions and restaurants and that children of any age be allowed to drink at home under parental supervision. Engs maintains that the reason American teenagers abuse alcohol is that they see it as a "forbidden fruit"; because drinking is illegal, it seems more appealing, and so teens are likely to drink to excess. In an interview with Hanson, Engs explains: "The flaunting of the current age-specific prohibition is readily apparent among young people who, since the increase in the minimum legal drinking age, have tended to drink in a more [abusive] manner than do those of legal age."

However, the argument that the European attitude toward alcohol is healthier is widely questioned. In its paper "Minimum Legal Drinking Age: Facts and Fallacies," the American Medical Association reports that alcohol-related problems such as cirrhosis occur in Europe at a rate similar to or higher than in the United States. Drunk driving accidents are less common, but that is because "European youth must be older to obtain their drivers' licenses, are less likely to have a car, and are more inclined to use public transportation." Also questioned is the longstanding belief that Jews are less prone to alcoholism. Dr. Abraham Twerski, medical director of the Gateway Rehabilitation Center, notes that the problem of alcoholism might be ignored in the Jewish community. Twerski argues: "[Alcohol and substance abuse] is the kind of thing that nobody talks about. The Jewish population tries to cover it up."

The notion that parents should permit their teenagers to drink at home is also called into question by some researchers. In particular, the argument that parents are the best people to teach adolescents about drinking, because they will be most concerned about the welfare of their children, is disputed. Some parents supervise parties for their children where alcohol is consumed. However, such behavior can have serious consequences. It is illegal to purchase alcohol for a minor (other than one's own children), and adults who do so could be financially and legally liable if a minor has an alcohol-related accident. In worst case scenarios, teenagers have gotten into fatal car accidents or nearly died from alcohol poisoning at adult-supervised gatherings. According to the Alcohol Epidemiology Program (AEP), a research program at the University of Minnesota in Minneapolis, "One study found that teens whose parents or friend's parents provided alcohol for parties were more likely to: drink, drink heavily, get in traffic crashes, be involved in violence and participate in thefts."

Instead, the AEP and others argue, parents should be sure to restrict their children's access to alcohol and make it clear that it should only be consumed by adults—and then never to excess. Parents are encouraged to communicate with other parents to be sure that alcohol will not be served at their childrens' parties and teach their children how to say "no" if alcohol is offered to them. In "Growing Up Drug Free: A Parent's Guide to Prevention," the U.S. Department of Education tells parents:

> Recognize how your actions affect the development of your child's values. Simply stated, children copy their parent's behavior. . . . Consider how your attitudes and actions may be shaping your child's choice about whether or not to use alcohol or other drugs.

> This does not mean, however, that if you are in the habit of having wine with dinner or an occasional beer or cocktail you must stop. Children can understand and accept that there are differences between what adults may do legally and what is appropriate and legal for children. Keep that distinction sharp, however. Do not let your children be involved in your drinking by mixing a cocktail for you or bringing you a beer, and do not allow your child to have sips of your drink.

If a parent is an alcoholic, it might be even more important that his or her child not be exposed to alcohol. Studies suggest that alcoholism is genetic—compared to the general population, children of alcoholics are three to four times more likely to become alcoholics.

One argument in favor of keeping the minimum legal drinking age (MLDA) at 21 is that the later a person starts drinking, the less likely he or she will become an alcoholic. If the MLDA is lowered to 18 or 19, some people assert, younger teenagers will find it even easier to obtain alcohol from their older friends and siblings. Carolyn Rosenfeld contends in *Alcohol Health & Research World* that arguments against age-21 drinking laws are misinformed. She writes: "A common argument among opponents of a higher MLDA is that because many minors still drink and purchase alcohol, an MLDA of 21 does not work. The evidence shows, however, that although many youth still consume alcohol, they drink less and experience fewer alcohol-related injuries and deaths than they did under lower MLDA's."

While the influence of parents and culture can be critical, they are not the only reasons why teenagers might develop alcohol-related problems. The behavior of peers and television advertisements can also lead to teenage alcohol abuse. In *Teen Alcoholism: Contemporary Issues Companion*, the contributors consider not only the causes of teen alcoholism, but also its effects on health and families and how it can be reduced or prevented.

CHAPTER 1

THE CAUSES OF TEEN ALCOHOLISM

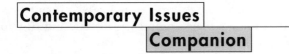

Contemporary Issues
Companion

RISK FACTORS OF TEEN ALCOHOL USE

National Institute on Alcohol Abuse and Alcoholism

In the following selection, the National Institute on Alcohol Abuse and Alcoholism (NIAAA) explains how a variety of factors can lead to alcohol abuse among teenagers. The institute reports that teenagers with alcoholic parents are more likely to develop alcoholism. Other vulnerable teenagers include those with psychiatric disorders, those who have peers who drink, or those who have suffered physical or sexual abuse during childhood. The NIAAA supports and conducts biomedical and behavioral research on alcoholism and alcohol-related problems.

Despite a minimum legal drinking age of 21, many young people in the United States consume alcohol. Some abuse alcohol by drinking frequently or by binge drinking—often defined as having five or more drinks in a row. A minority of youth may meet the *Diagnostic and Statistical Manual of Mental Disorders, Fourth Edition* (DSM-IV) criteria for alcohol dependence. The progression of drinking from use to abuse to dependence is associated with biological and psychosocial factors. This [article] examines some of these factors that put youth at risk for drinking and for alcohol-related problems and considers some of the consequences of their drinking.

Prevalence of Youth Drinking

Thirteen- to fifteen-year-olds are at high risk to begin drinking. According to results of an annual survey of students in 8th, 10th, and 12th grades, 26 percent of 8th graders, 40 percent of 10th graders, and 51 percent of 12th graders reported drinking alcohol within the past month. Binge drinking at least once during the 2 weeks before the survey was reported by 16 percent of 8th graders, 25 percent of 10th graders, and 30 percent of 12th graders.

Males report higher rates of daily drinking and binge drinking than females, but these differences are diminishing. White students report the highest levels of drinking, blacks report the lowest, and Hispanics fall between the two.

A survey focusing on the alcohol-related problems experienced by 4,390 high school seniors and dropouts found that within the preced-

Excerpted from National Institute on Alcohol Abuse and Alcoholism, "Youth Drinking: Risk Factors and Consequences," *Alcohol Alert*, July 1997.

ing year, approximately 80 percent reported either getting "drunk," binge drinking, or drinking and driving. More than half said that drinking had caused them to feel sick, miss school or work, get arrested, or have a car crash.

Some adolescents who drink later abuse alcohol and may develop alcoholism. Although these conditions are defined for adults in the DSM, research suggests that separate diagnostic criteria may be needed for youth.

Drinking and Adolescent Development

While drinking may be a singular problem behavior for some, research suggests that for others it may be an expression of general adolescent turmoil that includes other problem behaviors and that these behaviors are linked to unconventionality, impulsiveness, and sensation seeking.

Binge drinking, often beginning around age 13, tends to increase during adolescence, peak in young adulthood (ages 18–22), then gradually decrease. In a 1994 national survey, binge drinking was reported by 28 percent of high school seniors, 41 percent of 21- to 22-year-olds, but only 25 percent of 31- to 32-year-olds. Individuals who increase their binge drinking from age 18 to 24 and those who consistently binge drink at least once a week during this period may have problems attaining the goals typical of the transition from adolescence to young adulthood (e.g., marriage, educational attainment, employment, and financial independence).

Risk Factors for Adolescent Alcohol Use

Genetic Risk Factors. Animal studies and studies of twins and adoptees demonstrate that genetic factors influence an individual's vulnerability to alcoholism. Children of alcoholics are significantly more likely than children of nonalcoholics to initiate drinking during adolescence and to develop alcoholism, but the relative influences of environment and genetics have not been determined and vary among people.

Biological Markers. Brain waves elicited in response to specific stimuli (e.g., a light or sound) provide measures of brain activity that predict risk for alcoholism. P300, a wave that occurs about 300 milliseconds after a stimulus, is most frequently used in this research. A low P300 amplitude has been demonstrated in individuals with increased risk for alcoholism, especially sons of alcoholic fathers. P300 measures among 36 preadolescent boys were able to predict alcohol and other drug (AOD) use 4 years later, at an average age of 16.

Childhood Behavior. Children classified as "undercontrolled" (i.e., impulsive, restless, and distractible) at age 3 were twice as likely as those who were "inhibited" or "well-adjusted" to be diagnosed with alcohol dependence at age 21. Aggressiveness in children as young as ages 5–10 has been found to predict AOD use in adolescence. Childhood antisocial behavior is associated with alcohol-related problems in adolescence and alcohol abuse or dependence in adulthood.

Psychiatric Disorders. Among 12- to 16-year-olds, regular alcohol use has been significantly associated with conduct disorder; in one study, adolescents who reported higher levels of drinking were more likely to have conduct disorder [a condition in which children repeatedly violate personal and property rights].

Six-year-old to seventeen-year-old boys with attention deficit hyperactivity disorder (ADHD) who were also found to have weak social relationships had significantly higher rates of alcohol abuse and dependence 4 years later, compared with ADHD boys without social deficiencies and boys without ADHD. [ADHD's symptoms include hyperactivity, poor attention span, and weak impulse control.]

Whether anxiety and depression lead to or are consequences of alcohol abuse is unresolved. In a study of college freshmen, a *Diagnostic and Statistical Manual of Mental Disorders, Third Edition* (DSM-III) diagnosis of alcohol abuse or dependence was twice as likely among those with anxiety disorder as those without this disorder. In another study, college students diagnosed with alcohol abuse were almost four times as likely as students without alcohol abuse to have a major depressive disorder. In most of these cases, depression preceded alcohol abuse. In a study of adolescents in residential treatment for AOD dependence, 25 percent met the DSM-III-R (revised) criteria for depression, three times the rate reported for controls. In 43 percent of these cases, the onset of AOD dependence preceded the depression; in 35 percent, the depression occurred first; and in 22 percent, the disorders occurred simultaneously.

Suicidal Behavior. Alcohol use among adolescents has been associated with considering, planning, attempting, and completing suicide. In one study, 37 percent of eighth-grade females who drank heavily reported attempting suicide, compared with 11 percent who did not drink. Research does not indicate whether drinking causes suicidal behavior, only that the two behaviors are correlated.

Psychological and Social Risks

Parenting, Family Environment, and Peers. Parents' drinking behavior and favorable attitudes about drinking have been positively associated with adolescents' initiating and continuing drinking. Early initiation of drinking has been identified as an important risk factor for later alcohol-related problems. Children who were warned about alcohol by their parents and children who reported being closer to their parents were less likely to start drinking.

Lack of parental support, monitoring, and communication have been significantly related to frequency of drinking, heavy drinking, and drunkenness among adolescents. Harsh, inconsistent discipline and hostility or rejection toward children have also been found to significantly predict adolescent drinking and alcohol-related problems.

Peer drinking and peer acceptance of drinking have been associated with adolescent drinking. While both peer influences and parental influences are important, their relative impact on adolescent drinking is unclear.

Expectancies. Positive alcohol-related expectancies have been identified as risk factors for adolescent drinking. Positive expectancies about alcohol have been found to increase with age and to predict the onset of drinking and problem drinking among adolescents.

Trauma. Child abuse and other traumas have been proposed as risk factors for subsequent alcohol problems. Adolescents in treatment for alcohol abuse or dependence reported higher rates of physical abuse, sexual abuse, violent victimization, witnessing violence, and other traumas compared with controls. The adolescents in treatment were at least 6 times more likely than controls to have ever been abused physically and at least 18 times more likely to have ever been abused sexually. In most cases, the physical or sexual abuse preceded the alcohol use. Thirteen percent of the alcohol dependent adolescents had experienced post-traumatic stress disorder, compared with 10 percent of those who abused alcohol and 1 percent of controls.

Advertising. Research on the effects of alcohol advertising on adolescent alcohol-related beliefs and behaviors has been limited. While earlier studies measured the effects of exposure to advertising, more recent research has assessed the effects of alcohol advertising awareness on intentions to drink. In a study of fifth- and sixth-grade students' awareness, measured by the ability to identify products in commercials with the product name blocked out, awareness had a small but statistically significant relationship to positive expectancies about alcohol and to intention to drink as adults. This suggests that alcohol advertising may influence adolescents to be more favorably predisposed to drinking.

Parental Drinking Contributes to Teen Alcoholism

Michael Windle

Michael Windle explains that adolescents whose parents have drinking problems are more likely to abuse alcohol. According to Windle, such parents tend to be less nurturing, which can lead their children to affiliate with friends who drink heavily. Additionally, alcoholic parents influence the behavior of their teenagers through role modeling; for example, children who see their parents using alcohol to cope with stress are likely to do the same. However, Windle explains, adolescents who have alcoholic parents can be protected against the potential of alcohol abuse if their family life is otherwise stable. Windle is a professor of psychology at the University of Alabama at Birmingham and a former senior research scientist at the Research Institute on Addictions in Buffalo.

Many biological, psychological, and social changes characterize the phase in the life span known as adolescence. These changes include the onset of puberty, an increased self-identity, the initiation of dating, and the development of intimate relationships. Early theories of adolescent development described this period as one of "storm and stress" with regard to parent-child relations. More recent research has indicated that adolescents confront a host of challenging and sometimes unique events. Although they frequently prefer to handle these challenges on their own, adolescents often view parents as significant confidants and social support agents in times of crises. Hence, although parents and adolescents may disagree over specific issues, such as curfew or amount of allowance, parents continue to play a salient role in the development of adolescents, just as they do with infants and young children. Problem drinking by parents, however, may disrupt this emerging pattern of parent-adolescent relations and adversely affect adolescent development and adjustment in several ways. . . .

Problem-drinking parents may provide lower levels of parental nurturing and emotional availability, thereby increasing the risk for ado-

Excerpted from Michael Windle, "Effect of Parental Drinking on Adolescents," *Alcohol Health & Research World*, Summer 1996.

lescent drinking. As mentioned previously, adolescents continue to rely on parents for emotional support to help with challenges, such as handling conflict with others, and for guidance in important future-oriented decisions. Higher levels of parental nurturance and warmth of expression consistently have been associated with lower levels of alcohol and substance use and higher levels of general mental health and well-being among adolescents. Parents who abuse alcohol typically provide less nurturance to their offspring. They are more often "emotionally unavailable" as a result of drinking-related consequences, which include hangovers, irritability, and negative mood states. These effects disrupt healthy emotional development in their children. To compensate for the lack of parental affection and support, adolescents may tend to affiliate with friends who drink more heavily. The child is thus propelled on a path of continual adverse outcomes. . . .

Problem-drinking parents frequently demonstrate a greater tolerance of adolescent drinking and other substance use. In this way, they provide implicit approval for their children's alcohol use. Research has consistently found that higher levels of parental tolerance of adolescent drinking are associated with an earlier onset of drinking among offspring as well as with the escalation to higher levels of alcohol use. Increased alcohol use, in turn, can lead to more alcohol-related adverse social consequences, such as problems at school or with legal authorities.

In addition to affecting parenting skills adversely, problem drinking by parents may negatively affect child and adolescent development by impairing marital and family relations. For example, higher levels of alcohol use by parents have been associated with higher levels of marital conflict. In turn, higher levels of marital conflict have been associated with higher levels of child and adolescent alcohol use and aggression. Marital conflict has a threatening and destabilizing influence on families. The fears of children in these families illustrate this effect; frequently, such children express concern both for the breakup of the family unit and for their personal safety. Prolonged marital conflict, influenced by parental alcohol use, may contribute to children's attempts to escape these aversive conditions through personal alcohol use with peers, who may be perceived as more emotionally supportive. . . .

How Parents Influence Adolescent Drinking

Parents may contribute to adolescent drinking even before the child is born by selecting a problem-drinking partner. This concept, described as "nonrandom partner selection" (i.e., assortative mating), refers to research findings indicating that alcoholics and problem drinkers are more likely to marry partners who abuse alcohol. Assortative mating may increase the likelihood of adverse outcomes among offspring by increasing both genetic and environmental risk. Genetic risk is increased because the offspring may inherit a genetic predisposition toward alcoholism through the combined lineages of the maternal and the paternal sides of the family. Environmental risk is increased in that the rearing environment of children raised by two alcoholic or problem-drinking parents may be severely compromised with regard to parenting skills, yielding a "double jeopardy" situation for the development of the offspring. In addition, if both parents have drinking problems, then the potential stress-buffering or moderating influences of a nondrinking parent are not present in the family. . . .

Problem-drinking parents may affect adolescent drinking through basic socialization and learning processes as well as through role modeling. Consistent positive associations between parental and adolescent levels of alcohol use have been reported in the research literature. Some researchers have suggested that many adolescents are simply imitating their parents' behavior because they see their parents as powerful figures to emulate. Other research has found that higher levels of parental alcohol use are associated with the earlier acquisition and elaboration of knowledge about alcohol use by children as young as preschool age. For instance, research has shown that preschool children with parents who drink alcohol are better able to identify alcoholic beverages (using a "blinded" smell test) than are preschoolers with parents who do not consume alcohol. Exposure to parental alcohol use also is associated with children's intentions to drink alcohol and their perception of alcohol consumption as a positive activity.

Parents who drink alcohol to cope with stressful life events also may affect their children through modeling an ineffective coping strategy. That is, children who observe self-medicating with alcohol in response to stress may perceive that such behavior is an effective way to confront distressing circumstances; they thus may be more likely to adopt the coping mechanism themselves. The difficulties with such a coping strategy are twofold. First, self-medicating with alcohol may provide short-term relief from "pressures," or stressors, but is not likely to be useful in generating constructive solutions that may ameliorate or eliminate the distress or its source. Second, adolescents' reliance on alcohol to self-medicate for depressed moods may contribute to more frequent and serious alcohol use and associated problems. These problems may, in turn, contribute to escalating levels of stressful life events (e.g., poorer school performance or contact with legal authorities) that may foster increased self-destructive use of alcohol.

Factors That Prevent Teen Alcoholism

Although much of the research literature has identified factors associated with parental problem drinking that negatively affect outcomes for children and adolescents, some research has attempted to identify family (and non-family) factors that "protect" high-risk children, such as children of alcoholics, from adverse outcomes. For example, S.J.

Wolin and colleagues (1979) reported that families with alcoholic members who retained relatively stable patterns of behavior around everyday activities, such as meals, and the celebration of special events, such as births, marriages, and holidays (i.e., family rituals) had offspring with higher levels of adjustment and fewer alcohol problems than did families whose family rituals were disrupted by the alcoholic family member. Hence, the preservation of family rituals provided more stability, predictability, and perceived support for these offspring.

Other family related protective factors include the strength of positive emotional ties (e.g., warmth and nurturance) with family members, consistent and fair rules for adolescent conduct, and "open" parent-child communication styles. The emotional strength of the parent-child relationship has been related to delays in the age of onset of substance use and to a decreased probability of escalation to more serious levels of use. Similarly, parental monitoring of, and clear and fair guidelines for, adolescent behaviors (e.g., with regard to curfew or household tasks) have been associated with lower levels of alcohol and other substance use and with a less deviant peer network. Parent-child communication plays a significant role both in establishing and maintaining positive emotional ties and in promoting mutual understanding of rules of conduct. Adolescents are more likely to communicate openly with parents if they believe that they will not be criticized and belittled. Likewise, open discussion regarding adolescent conduct (e.g., curfew) may facilitate understanding (if not agreement) by adolescents and perhaps a greater sense of involvement and participation in decisions that directly affect their lives.

Adolescent behaviors, including alcohol use and abuse, are influenced by a multitude of biological, psychological, and sociocultural factors. Furthermore, not all adolescents are influenced by the same set of factors. For some problem-drinking adolescents, parental role-modeling behaviors may be more influential, whereas for others, disrupted family relations (e.g., marital conflict) may have more influence. In addition, current knowledge is limited with regard to how adolescent drinking behavior is related to adult alcohol abuse or other manifestations of maladjustment (e.g., depression or criminality). Nevertheless, it is evident that parental alcohol abuse may have a range of potential adverse effects on adolescents. Problem drinking by parents may influence role-modeling behaviors, parenting skills, and marital and family relations, all of which may contribute to a host of problematic outcomes for adolescents. Without appropriate parent-child or family based interventions, these disruptive, alcohol-influenced parenting behaviors may contribute to internalizing problems (e.g., depression and anxiety disorders) and externalizing problems (e.g., delinquency) among children and adolescents, including early onset of alcohol use and a rapid acceleration to problematic use throughout adolescence and into adulthood.

American Attitudes Toward Alcohol Lead to Underage Drinking

Dwight B. Heath

In the following selection, Dwight B. Heath suggests that America's excessively temperate attitudes toward alcohol cause underage drinking. He argues that because alcohol is seen as a "forbidden fruit," adolescents are more likely to be tempted to drink to excess. In contrast, societies in which individuals are introduced to alcohol at an early age and taught how to drink moderately have lower rates of alcohol dependence. Heath is a professor emeritus of anthropology at Brown University in Providence, Rhode Island, and the author of *Drinking Occasions: Comparative Perspectives on Alcohol and Culture.*

Early [in 2000] the American print media amply reported another in a long trail of negative announcements regarding alcoholic beverage consumption. The press release that had triggered this wave of alcohol reportage, with its somber extrapolations, had grown out of a research project sponsored by the U.S. National Institute on Alcohol Abuse and Alcoholism (NIAAA). This study, published in the *Journal of Substance Abuse,* had concerned the correlation of (1) age of first beverage alcohol intake and (2) alcoholism. Its principal finding was, in simple terms, that subjects who had first imbibed at an early age were, to a statistically significant degree, likelier eventually to become alcoholics than were those who hadn't.

It is no secret that correlation often has little bearing on causation, yet many print journalists treated this finding as if it were dramatic proof that alcoholic beverage consumption is highly addictive and that it is dangerous for anyone under age 21. The same finding might be counterintuitive to anyone conversant with life in modern Europe or among Orthodox Jews. In Europe, frequently individuals are first invited to drink at an early age, but rates of alcohol dependence tend to be very low. Orthodox Jewish males are commonly given a taste of

Reprinted from Dwight B. Heath, "Should We 'Just Say No' to Childhood Drinking?" *Priorities for Health,* 2000. Reprinted with permission from *Priorities,* a publication of the American Council on Science and Health (ACSH), 1995 Broadway, 2nd Floor, New York, NY 10023-5800. Learn more about ACSH online at www.acsh.org or www.prioritiesforhealth.com.

wine on the occasion of their circumcision—eight days after their birth. And many followers of that faith—youngsters as well as adults—drink wine ceremonially at least twice a week. But rates of drinking-related problems among Orthodox Jews are remarkably low.

A Counterproductive Movement

Indeed, the NIAAA finding does not apply in most parts of the world outside the United States—where, alas, the finding is altogether reasonable. At least some of the efforts of the new temperance movement—i.e., the efforts of a loose, variegated coalition of activists trying to reduce beverage-alcohol consumption by humans categorically—evidently have been counterproductive.

Childhood drinking is deviant in the U.S.; in many states it is also illegal. One would reasonably expect that in such a setting underage drinkers would consist almost entirely of persons who freely behave in other deviant (e.g., risky or illegal) ways, in some cases deliberately. By the same token, one would reasonably expect that law-abiding, conformist youngsters who tend to avoid risks would also tend to defer drinking at least until adulthood. In other words, it is almost certainly not adolescent or childhood drinking per se that leads to adulthood drinking problems; it is far likelier that factors that predispose children and adolescents to deviant drinking and to other such behaviors are responsible.

Yet advocates of the new temperance movement have structured the relationship in the U.S. between childhood drinking and adulthood drinking problems so that the former phenomenon appears almost always to result in the latter!

Different Attitudes Toward Alcohol

In most parts of the world, beverage alcohol lacks the "forbidden fruit" appeal that invites its use by youngsters as a demonstration of maturity and/or as a means of becoming sociable, sexy, dynamic, or more powerful. Where children are not "protected from alcohol," their behavior suggests no need for such protection. These children take up drinking in relatively supportive surroundings (usually in their homes and among adult members of their families) as a wholesome and enjoyable part of everyday life—rather than as an illicit, surreptitious consequence of peer pressure.

As an anthropologist, I often deal with patterns of populations that are small, isolated, or tribal and whose characteristic beliefs and behaviors would not be feasible in industrial or post-industrial communities. But some of the best illustrations of my case concern the present-day middle classes of France, Italy, Spain, and other developed countries. Through official statistics from such countries, on such well-studied communities, I have repeatedly demonstrated that the incidence of so-called alcohol-related problems (physiological, psychological, social, economic, etc.) is inversely related both to "age of onset" (i.e., how early in one's life one first imbibes) and to average per capita consumption of beverage alcohol. This is just the opposite of what is claimed by the World Health Organization, the NIAAA, and other organizations primarily concerned with restricting alcoholic-beverage availability as a public health policy.

The same climate that almost guarantees that underage American drinkers will be otherwise deviant and will flout the law also virtually ensures that they will often drink furtively and excessively or rashly, and that they will do so among peers ignorant or unmindful of the specific long- and short-term risks of alcohol abuse—peers who may be reluctant to summon an adult in the event of an acute problem.

The "Just Say No" approach thus invites troubles.

The Advantages of Early Socialization

In communities in which early socialization to drinking is the norm (i.e., in most communities), youngsters learn simultaneously how to drink moderately, how and why to avoid drunkenness, that drinking will not magically improve one's personality, and that excessive drinking illustrates weakness.

In short, the theory that early drinking leads to drinking problems is correct—but only in those few communities in which the normative and legal systems make the theory correct.

For anyone for whom such cross-cultural evidence is not compelling, I recommend reading an article whose authors used a statistical methodology similar to that used by most of those who publish in support of the above-mentioned theory: "Age at First Drink and Risk for Alcoholism: A Noncausal Association," published [in 1999] in the prestigious journal Alcoholism: Clinical and Experimental Research.

Social Pressures Encourage Teen Drinking

Sharon Scott, LPC, LMFT

In the following essay, Sharon Scott contends that pressures from the media and from peers can lead to alcohol problems for many teenagers. She writes that due to the increasingly high-tech and urban aspects of modern society, children are constantly bombarded with negative messages that encourage alcohol use and other harmful behaviors. These messages are becoming more powerful because families communicate less than they did in the past, Scott contends, thus reducing the influence of parents on children's behavior. Scott suggests that parents teach their children how to understand and respond to peer pressure in order to make the right decisions about alcohol. Scott is a professional counselor and the author of several books, including *How to Say No and Keep Your Friends: Peer Pressure Reversal for Teens & Preteens.*

Myth: Alcohol is not a problem with today's youth.

Fact: Ninety-one percent of high-school seniors have tried alcohol, with an estimated 3.3 million teenage alcoholics.

Myth: Youth are so well educated on drugs that they know alcohol use is harmful.

Fact: Fifty-six percent of high-school seniors think that five or more drinks once or twice a weekend is not harmful.

Myth: Youthful drinking is just the way things are today. They will quit heavy drinking by the time they get out of college.

Fact: In too many instances youthful drinking habits persist through life. A *Reader's Digest*/Gallup Survey indicates that the proportion of moderate-to-heavy drinkers did finally drop by two-thirds, but not until around age 30. Of adults who drink, some 7 to 10 percent will become chronic alcoholics, generally within 15–20 years. Of juveniles who drink, the odds for alcoholism are two or three times as high.

Myth: Booze will keep them from trying other drugs.

Fact: Early use of alcohol is associated with increased involvement in other drug use. Sixty-three percent of young heavy drinkers reported using marijuana during the previous month, while only 4 percent of those who abstain from alcohol use pot.

Myth: Peer pressure has always been around. It could not have that much effect on kids' decisions to drink.

Fact: Drinking is now an expected party activity in youthful social circles of all economic levels. The average age for the first drink is now 11½ years old—and dropping. A 1983 *Weekly Reader* survey of children ages 9 to 12 showed that almost half reported peer pressure to drink. In a Stanford University School of Medicine survey, substance use by peers is the most significant factor influencing the participants' increased level of use. And in a Colorado State University study of 350 midwestern 11th and 12th graders, Fred Beauvais found friends' habits have at least five times more impact than other lifestyle factors on teen drug use.

The Dangers of Alcohol

Alcohol has been called the most active drug affecting the human body, impairing the intellect, physical abilities, and metabolism. The chemical action of alcohol is similar to that of ether. Ethyl alcohol (ethanol), the substance in beverage alcohol which produces intoxication, is a drug in the same chemical class as tranquilizers and barbiturates.

Alcohol use by youth has devastating consequences. Young people between the ages of 15 and 24 are the only group in America with a declining life expectancy. Driving under the influence is the leading cause of death for teens. Suicide is the second major cause of teenage deaths, and today such suicides are ten times more likely to be alcohol or other drug related than they were 20 years ago. Approximately 10,000 young people ages 16 to 24 are killed each year in other types of alcohol-related accidents, including drownings, violent injuries, homicides, and inhalation of vomit. And the National Campus Violence Survey found that alcohol factored into four of ten sexual assaults at the schools surveyed. All 1988 sexual assaults at the University of Colorado were alcohol-related. The most common ingredients for a gang rape are a freshman girl, a party, and lots of alcohol.

Children Receive Harmful Messages

The changes in our society during the past 30 years challenge both children and adults. Unfortunately, today's high-tech lifestyle is reducing the quality of adult-child interactions while increasing the negative messages to children. Children are growing up faster than at any previous time. Between 1935 and 1950, the greatest social change ever known in the U.S. took place. By 1950, census reports showed that 70 percent of all Americans lived in an urban environment with only 30 percent on farms—a complete reversal of the 1935 statistic. By 1970, 90 percent of Americans lived in an urban environment.

Thus, in just 35 years, Americans made the transition which had taken nearly 400 years in Europe.

Children are growing up faster than at any previous time. Difficult decisions once made in the late teens are now routinely made by children in elementary school. Elementary children are frequently allowed to attend all-night group slumber parties, go to malls with friends (no adults), dress like miniature adults, and even begin boyfriend-girlfriend relationships.

Images are communicated and substances are made available more widely to the masses than ever before. Many of those images and substances are too adult, or harmful, for children, and go against family values. Weight is given to alcohol and other drug use, violence, dishonesty, selfishness, beauty by biased and merely physical standards, other poor morals, and unhealthful sexuality. Children receive these messages from the many technetronic media: television, videos, movies, radio, live entertainment, magazines, books, and advertisements.

From the media children learn more at earlier ages, and of course imitate what they see. The media also reinforce peer pressure: if you want to have a good personality and be popular, you have to drink alcohol, wear a certain brand, or use a particular toothpaste, for instance, or else you won't be a part of the "in" group. This puts a lot of pressure on parents trying to raise children with their own sound values. . . .

Isolation Can Leave Children Vulnerable

Television not only force-feeds unhealthful messages to children, but it also contributes heavily to this isolation within the home. In the 1950s, when television watching became widespread, families reduced their shared communication and recreation.

Meals had always been the primary time for family communication, but TV has given "prime time" a different direction. The family now tends to "graze" in shifts. Too often the time saved with microwave ovens and other technology isn't being put back into parenting and family interaction. Today's parents spend too much time working for external success and a higher standard of living and not enough time developing responsible children.

What communication a family does have tends to be of poor quality. The most interaction at home often bears the anxious or sour tone of fussing, nagging, and lecturing. This poor communication is a result of parents having little time for doing more than keeping order, because it's easy to notice the negative while taking the good for granted.

Another weakening in the child's support system is the decline of the "extended family"—nonparent adults in the family—which is on the "endangered species" list and fast becoming extinct. Extra adults around the child can provide an additional helping of attention and guidance, which encourages the child's responsible behavior and good self-image, while at the same time supports the parents' parallel efforts. At a similar rate, families are splitting into single-parent homes.

Often there are no friendships with neighbors. Traditionally, neighbors and relatives helped to guard children through a community spirit. The community puts healthful pressure for good social values on everyone, at the risk of social ostracism.

All of these changes in society converge to leave children unprecedently vulnerable to public pressure, especially peer pressure, which is so close to "home" and which is often substituted for family influence.

How to Deal with Peer Pressure

Being aware of these societal changes also helps parents see how urgent it is that their children learn to deal with negative peer pressure. The best method for this is the practical, proven effective, decision-making skill called "Peer Pressure Reversal" (PPR), taught to over one million youth from kindergarten to college. Once he or she has learned PPR, the average child uses it within 24 hours. If a child has difficulty saying "No" on small decisions for fear of losing friends, given the right circumstances that same fear can cause a child who knows better to take alcohol or other drugs.

A parent should not assume that just knowing right from wrong and being told to say "No" will enable his or her child to manage negative peer pressure. If children are not taught how to say "No" and still save face with their friends, they will frequently go along with their peers. Youth say it is especially hard to say "No" to best friends, older or popular youth, and boy or girl friends. Youth tend to value social worth over themselves and sometimes over safety. Peer pressure situations are everywhere—the solution is not in changing neighborhoods or schools, but in giving youth the ability to make difficult, often adult, decisions.

Saying "No" in the face of negative peer pressure is one of the most important things parents can teach youth—as simple as it might seem it is also one of the most difficult.

What is peer pressure? It is the encouragement of a person toward another of similar age to think or act the same way. Peer pressure can be positive, such as encouraging a classmate to study for a test or cheering for a teammate; or negative, involving decisions that are wrong, dangerous, harmful, or illegal.

Peer pressure can begin when a child is about four years old. A person might hear one child saying to another, "I'm mad at Shawn. Don't talk to him or you're not my friend!" Even at this age, the child will be torn over how to handle this situation. Wanting to maintain the friendship, the child probably does what the friend asks. But no matter what the child does, he or she feels bad and thus a cycle of damaged self-esteem and control by peers begins and can escalate to more serious decisions such as talking in class, copying homework, gossiping, vandalism, sneaking out of the house, stealing, prank phone calls, skipping school, and so on. By the time the child reaches junior high, he or she will be facing some of the most difficult decisions of his or her life about alcohol and other drug use.

ADVERTISING MAY ENCOURAGE TEEN ALCOHOL CONSUMPTION

Alcohol Policies Project

Teenagers see numerous advertisements for alcoholic beverages on television or in magazines. In the following selection, the Alcohol Policies Project details the results of a study on how adolescents respond to five beer commercials that portray alcohol as a product that brings friends and couples together. While results are not wholly conclusive, the study suggests that teenagers may be encouraged to drink as a result of the commercials. Many teenagers believe that these advertisements encourage underage drinking, the study found, but they also recognize that the commercials present beer consumption in an overly positive light. The project notes that children of alcoholics are more likely to anticipate both positive and negative outcomes from drinking. The Alcohol Policies Project, an offshoot of the Center for Science in the Public Interest, advocates policy reforms that will help reduce the health and social consequences of drinking.

By the time they reach the age of 21, American youth see thousands of advertisements for alcoholic beverages—mostly for beer—on television. These ads often glamorize drinking and position beer as an important consumer product. With the exception of public service ads denouncing drinking and driving, few, if any, beer advertisements provide information about the potential negative consequences of its use.

In 1994, brewers spent $588.8 million advertising their products on television, much of it on the sponsorship of televised sporting events and other programming routinely watched by adolescents. Television advertising amounted to 83% of all beer advertising expenditures in the mass media and 59% of all spending for alcoholic-beverage ads. Beer ads often feature youth-oriented themes, characters, and activities, including athletic competition and recreation, beach and street parties, socializing, and humor. Recently, many beer ads have featured animated animals that have clear appeal to young people.

Whether these ads affect youth consumption of alcohol or influ-

Excerpted from Alcohol Policies Project, "Adolescent Responses to Televised Beer Advertisements: Children of Alcoholics and Others," available at www.cspinet.org/booze/beeradvertisements.htm. Reprinted with permission from the Center for Science in the Public Interest.

ence the attitudes young people develop about beer has been hotly debated by researchers, health activists, and representatives of the alcoholic-beverage industry. In all likelihood, it may not be possible to demonstrate a causal relationship between alcohol advertising and consumption; not because the relationship doesn't exist, but because current research methodology is unable to measure that connection.

Previous studies of the effects of alcohol advertising on young people have attempted to determine the impact advertisements have on alcohol consumption patterns and attitudes toward drinkers and alcohol. Surprisingly, there has been no research on the effects of exposure to alcohol advertising on children of alcoholics, a population at particularly high risk of alcohol dependence.

This pilot study set out to compare the responses of adolescent children of alcoholics and other adolescents to televised beer commercials. Since children of alcoholics have been exposed to extensive parental alcohol abuse and dependence, our purpose was to explore their potential vulnerability to the advertisements and assess the need for and direction of additional research in this area. Is parental alcoholism related to the way young people process images in beer advertising? Are children of alcoholics immune to messages of beer advertisements because of their own personal experiences? Are they especially vulnerable? . . .

Evaluating Five Commercials

To measure adolescents' perceptions of drinking and television beer advertising, we designed a short questionnaire and assembled a video of five television beer commercials. . . .

Commercial #1: Budweiser Rookie Construction Worker—This 60-second ad features a young apprentice being selected for a construction job assignment, putting in a hard day's work with more experienced workers, and then going to a bar for a drink afterwards. One of the older workers signals acceptance of the rookie by inviting him for a beer.

Commercial #2: Miller Genuine Draft Fantasy Island—This ad depicts a crowded beach on a hot day. A man singles out an attractive female sunbather and creates a deserted island for the two of them by pouring water from his boot in a circle around her. He pulls out a beer and the two of them embrace, alone on the island.

Commercial #3: Bud Light Beach Play—This ad features beach scenes, with attractive young men and women enjoying Bud Light beer as they ride bikes, swim, and talk with friends.

Commercial #4: St. Ides Rapper—In this malt-liquor commercial, popular rapper Ice Cube stands on an inner-city street holding a 40-ounce bottle of St. Ides. Using MTV-style videography, additional urban youth appear in the background as Ice Cube raps about drinking St. Ides.

Commercial #5: Miller Lite TV Drinking Party—The fantasy-based ad depicts a couple unable to watch television because every channel shows Miller Lite. The television repairman tells them they need to drain the beer from the set, and suggests they invite friends over. The result is a party with the television set functioning as a beer keg. . . .

Analysis of the data did not reveal many differences in responses to beer advertisements by children of alcoholics and other adolescents. However, in several areas, children of alcoholics indicated a disturbing vulnerability to the messages delivered by the ads. This section summarizes the key findings for all respondents and highlights troublesome differences in responses based on age and exposure to parental alcohol abuse and dependence.

Ads Depict Heavy Drinking

For each of the five beer commercials, respondents were asked how many beers the characters would consume. Alarmingly, most adolescents perceived a high level of alcohol consumption in the advertisements, irrespective of the nature of character portrayals and imagery in the ads. Adolescent viewers indicated that ad characters consumed an average of 3.7 beers in a single advertisement. Many youth estimated that the characters were binge drinking—five or more beers.

| | Perceived beer consumption | | |
| | *number of beers consumed* | | |
Commercial	0–2	3–4	5 or more
Budweiser Rookie Construction Worker	17%	43%	40%
Miller Genuine Draft Fantasy Island	34	34	32
Bud Light Beach Play	29	32	39
St. Ides Rapper	20	32	48
Miller Lite TV Drinking Party	6	26	68

The *Miller Lite TV Drinking Party* ad elicited particularly high estimates of the quantity of beers consumed. Sixty-eight percent of the respondents said characters in this ad would drink at least five beers, and another 15% estimated four. The *St. Ides Rapper* ad also elicited perceptions of heavy drinking by many respondents: 48% estimated binge drinking, and another 12% estimated the characters would drink four beers. In contrast, only 10% estimated that the rappers in this ad would drink two beers. Across all the ads, an average of only one-fifth (21%) of respondents said ad characters consumed two or fewer beers.

Children of alcoholics were vulnerable to perceptions of heavy drinking. For the *Budweiser Rookie Construction Worker* ad: 50% of the children of alcoholics said they thought characters would drink five or more beers, compared to 37% of the other respondents. Similarly, 44% of children of alcoholics thought the characters in the *Bud Light Beach Play* ad would consume five or more beers, compared to 37% of the other children, although this latter finding was not statistically significant.

Younger viewers were also more likely to perceive excessive drinking. Forty-four percent (44%) of the younger respondents estimated consumption of five or more beers in the *Bud Light Beach Play* ad, compared to 34% of their older peers. On average, younger viewers estimated that characters in this ad would have 3.6 drinks, while older viewers estimated only 3.2.

Children of Alcoholics React Differently

While children of alcoholics may be drawn to the enjoyable stories and characters portrayed in the ads, they had difficulty reconciling these images with the reality of drinkers they know. After viewing the ads, respondents were asked to circle words that described their feelings about the ads and people they know who drink beer.

Although most respondents reported neutral or positive feelings, children of alcoholics were significantly more likely to report feeling confused, angry, sad, and embarrassed after watching the commercials. For example, 35% of the children from alcoholic families said they felt confused after viewing the *Miller Lite TV Drinking Party* ad, compared to only 24% of the other children. This same ad triggered feelings of sadness in 35% of the children of alcoholics, anger in 34% and embarrassment in 30%.

These feelings of confusion, sadness, anger, and embarrassment were also evidenced in the open-ended responses. A child of an alcoholic explained, "I really don't like any of these commercials. A person who drinks beer is stupid. . . . I don't think it's cool, I think it really sucks." Another disconcerted viewer wrote, "I really think that these commercials don't make sense. People are not always happy, beautiful or tough when they drink any alcohol."

Negative and Positive Consequences of Drinking

Although they tended to associate positive attributes with drinkers in ads, respondents were less optimistic in projecting how drinking the advertised brands would affect their own future lives. In fact, when asked if they'd "have more fun," "be less happy," "have more friends," or "have more problems with my family" because of drinking the

advertised beer, respondents overall were much more likely to anticipate negative than positive outcomes.

After viewing the *Miller Genuine Draft Fantasy Island* commercial,
62% of the survey participants said that drinking Miller would cause
them more problems with their families and 39% said they would be
less happy. Conversely, only about one-fifth (1/5) said they would
have more fun, more friends, and go out on more dates as a result of
drinking Miller beer.

One troubling finding revealed that while children from alcoholic
families were more likely to anticipate negative consequences of
drinking beer, they were also slightly more likely to anticipate positive outcomes than other children. For example, 22% of the children
of alcoholics said they would have more friends if they drank Miller
beer, compared to only 18% of the other youngsters; 24% said they
would go out on more dates (compared to only 16% of other teens).

Younger respondents were significantly more aware of the potential negative outcomes. For the *Miller Lite TV Drinking Party* ad, more
than half of the younger children anticipated fights, sadness, and few
friends as a result of drinking the brand. In contrast, only 24% of the
older respondents envisioned these results.

Adolescents Feel Targeted by Beer Ads

The beer industry claims to use actors in beer ads who are at least 25
years old; however, the study found that this may not significantly
reduce the appeal that the ads have for adolescent viewers. In
response to questions about the age of characters who appeared in the
ads, most adolescents recognized that actors in the alcohol advertisements were at least 21 years old. For all the ads, an average of only
15% thought that characters were under 21. This rose to 28% of viewers of the *St. Ides Rapper* ad.

Younger viewers, however, were twice as likely as older viewers to
believe that the actors were underage. On average, 20% thought the
actors were under 21. For the *Budweiser Rookie Construction Worker* ad,
24% of the younger viewers believed the actor was underage, compared to 14% of the older viewers. Younger adolescents were more
than twice as likely (32% to 15%) to think the characters in the *St.
Ides Rapper* ad were under 21. According to one younger viewer, "some
of the people in the commercials look around 17 and 18. Because of
this, people may think its cool to drink underage."

Although most adolescents in the study recognized that actors
were of legal drinking age, a large percentage of the respondents to
one ad (the *St. Ides Rapper*) indicated that the brewer intends for their
product to be consumed by young people. When asked at what age
the advertiser for this beer thinks people should start drinking, a star-
tling 77% of respondents estimated an age under 21.

This response indicates that using clearly adult characters in ads may not reduce their appeal to underage consumers. Regardless of the beer industry's policy to use only actors above the age of 25 in televised advertisements, adolescents still come away with the belief that they are being targeted by the companies. As one respondent explained in the open-ended comment section of the survey, "the companies are using older people, while obviously targeting younger people." Another young viewer remarked, "I think they are trying to get teenagers to drink beer so they will always buy beer." The belief that teenagers are the intended consumers of alcoholic beverages was consistent with the finding that more than 50% of the younger viewers agreed with the assertion that almost all teenagers drink alcohol.

Beer Ads Are Unrealistic

In order to sell their products, advertisements typically associate beer consumption with sexual prowess, athleticism, and social success, and show characters having fun in different social settings. To determine whether respondents came away from viewing the ads with favorable perceptions of characters, adolescents were asked to select words which described them.

While respondents' perceptions of the drinkers varied according to the storyline of the ads, in general, adolescents regarded drinkers they saw in the ads as having a positive array of characteristics. For example, respondents associated such qualities as "good-looking," "popular," "cool," "fun," and "happy," with characters in the beach ads ten times more than negative qualities such as "sad," "mean," "threatening," "loud," and "tired."

The strong positive traits viewers attributed to characters in beer ads contrasted markedly with their descriptions of beer drinkers in real life. In general, respondents ascribed many negative traits to beer drinkers they personally know. For example, when averaged across four ads:

- Sixty-eight percent (68%) indicated that drinkers in the ads appeared happy but only 42% associated this characteristic with drinkers they know;
- Thirteen percent (13%) associated angry with drinkers in the ads; 43% associated it with drinkers in real life;
- Thirteen percent (13%) said drinkers in the ads appeared tired; 42% said drinkers in real life were tired;
- Seven percent (7%) said drinkers in the ads were sad; 25% said real life drinkers were sad.

Children of alcoholics were more likely than their peers to ascribe both positive and negative traits to drinkers they know, with statistically significant differences for four traits: "cool" (41% of the children of alcoholics identified this as a trait of beer drinkers they know, compared to only 30% of other adolescents), "angry" (54% compared to

39%), "tough" (49% compared to 40%), and "mean" (49% compared to 42%). In contrast, they appeared to agree in general with young-sters from non-alcoholic families about how they perceived the char-acters in the ads.

Mixed Attitudes About Underage Drinking

Prior to viewing the commercials, respondents were asked whether they agreed with a series of statements about alcohol, teenagers, and drinking. Their responses varied dramatically. Many youths indicated approval of underage drinking. Twenty percent said that "it is accept-able for teenagers to get drunk," and one-third said that "teenagers should be able to drink."

At the conclusion of the survey, when asked at what age a person should be before starting to drink beer, 57% indicated an age under 21. "Drinking alcohol should be allowed to everyone over 13 years," explained one viewer. "There shouldn't be an age limit to be allowed to drink, maybe 13 or something," remarked another.

Perhaps even more revealing than the adolescents' own views of alcohol consumption were their perceptions of their friends' attitudes about underage drinking. While 36% of the respondents indicated that "getting drunk can be fun," 46% said that their "friends think getting drunk can be fun." Nearly half agreed with the statement that "almost all teenagers drink alcohol." Fifty percent said that their "friends drink alcohol a lot." Because many young teens are influ-enced by the normative behavior and attitudes of their peers, this finding should be of particular interest to professionals working with young people, communities, and parents.

Many other adolescents indicated strong disapproval of underage consumption. Comments such as "Alcohol stinks," "Alcohol is bad," "I don't ever want to drink," and "I think teenagers should not drink" were common in the open-ended responses.

Age appears to be a strong factor in approval of underage drinking. Younger respondents were significantly less likely than their older peers to think it acceptable for teens to get drunk. Only 26% of the 11–12 year olds, compared to 62% of the older participants, said it was "okay to drink heavily." Moreover, more than half of the older viewers reported that they, as well as their friends, think that "getting drunk is fun"; the younger adolescents were less than half as likely to agree. In addition, the 11–12 year olds were considerably less likely than the older respondents to state that "some kinds of alcohol taste good" and that "alcohol makes people feel relaxed" and "friendly."

Imaginative Ads Are More Appealing

The survey also included questions designed to determine what kinds of advertisements and characters appeal to young viewers. Respondents provided substantial information about their preferences through their answers to both closed and open-ended questions.

None of the five commercials elicited an overwhelmingly positive response. On average, only 23% said they liked the ads a lot, and 35% said they liked the ads a little. The most appealing of the five was the romantic *Miller Genuine Draft Fantasy Island* ad, with 77% reporting liking it a lot or a little. Two ads which featured people socializing were also well received: the *Bud Light Beach Play* ad was liked by 67% of respondents, and the fantasy-based *Miller Lite TV Drinking Party* scored 66%.

In contrast, only 35% of the adolescent viewers reported that they liked the *Budweiser Rookie Construction Worker* ad. Age and history of parental alcoholism were not related to preferences for ads.

Viewer approval of beer advertisements appears to be related directly to the fantasy-like quality of the character portrayals. The more imaginative and romantic the character portrayal, the higher the viewer approval rating. For instance, only 41% of the respondents thought that the characters in the most well-liked commercial, the *Miller Genuine Draft Fantasy Island* ad, were like people they knew, and just 44% rated the characters as realistic in the second-most popular ad—*Bud Light Beach Play*. In contrast, 72% of the respondents thought that characters in the *Budweiser Rookie Construction Worker* ad were realistic; it was their least favorite of the five commercials.

Viewers also expressed their preference for imaginative commercials in the open response section of the survey. Of all ads spontaneously mentioned, adolescents most frequently referred to Budweiser beer ads featuring animated, croaking frogs. "Some of the ads make no sense, but look cool like the Budweiser frogs. These catch the viewer's eye," explained one respondent. "If I do watch them [beer ads], it's because they are funny, like the frog Budweiser commercial," added another viewer. These unsolicited references to specific commercials indicate clearly that the Budweiser frog advertising campaign has been effective in attracting the attention of young people.

While respondents in general did not perceive that characters are like real people, younger teens were more susceptible to the fantasy. For example, 52% of the 11–12 year olds rated the *Miller Genuine Draft Fantasy Island* ad characters as realistic, compared to only 30% of the older respondents.

The data also indicate that the more children liked the advertisements, the more likely they were to have favorable attitudes towards drinking, as measured by agreement with such statements as: "it is easier to have fun at a party if you're drinking," "getting drunk can be fun," "alcohol makes drinkers feel friendly," and "almost all teenagers drink alcohol."

ADVERTISING DOES NOT ENCOURAGE TEEN ALCOHOL ABUSE

David J. Hanson

Alcohol advertisements do not encourage alcohol abuse among teenagers and may in fact have a positive influence, David J. Hanson argues in the following selection. Hanson contends that there is little, if any, connection between advertisements and alcohol consumption and that youths are more likely to see drinking during television programs than during commercials. According to Hanson, television commercials may actually encourage teenagers to have responsible attitudes toward alcohol by presenting the beverages as mundane products rather than evil temptations. Hanson is a sociology professor at the State University of New York at Potsdam and the author of *Alcohol Education: What We Must Do.*

Advertising increases alcohol consumption, which increases alcohol abuse. . . . Right? WRONG. There is no solid evidence from either scientific research or practical experience that this theory of advertising is correct.

Alcohol Advertising Does Not Affect Consumption

• A study by the Federal Trade Commission found that there is "no reliable basis to conclude that alcohol advertising significantly affects consumption, let alone abuse."

• A United States Senate subcommittee reported in the *Congressional Record* that it could not find evidence to conclude that advertising influences non-drinkers to begin drinking or to increase consumption.

• The United States Department of Health and Human Services in its report to Congress concluded that there is no significant relationship between alcohol advertising and alcohol consumption. Not surprisingly, it did not recommend banning or imposing additional restrictions on advertising.

• A University of Texas study of alcohol advertising over a 21-year period found that the amount of money spent on alcohol ads had little relationship with total consumption in the population.

Reprinted from David J. Hanson, "Advertising, Consumption, and Abuse," available at www2.potsdam.edu/alcohol-info/Advertising/Advertising.html. Reprinted with permission from the author.

- Studies in both Canada and the United States find no significant link between restrictions on advertising and alcohol consumption.
- Alcohol advertising expenditures have increased, during which time alcohol-related traffic fatalities have declined.
- The founding director of the National Institute on Alcohol Abuse and Alcoholism recently pointed out that "There is not a single study—not one study in the United States or internationally—that credibly connects advertising with an increase in alcohol use or abuse."
- The definitive review of research from around the world found that advertising has virtually no influence on consumption and has no impact whatsoever on either experimentation with alcohol or its abuse. This is consistent with other reviews of the research.
- Advertising does not increase consumption. For example, alcohol brand advertising was first introduced in New Zealand in 1992. While advertising continues to increase, consumption continues to fall.

The Purpose of Advertising

If advertising doesn't increase consumption, why bother to advertise? The answer is simple: to increase market share.

Alcohol is a "mature" product category in that consumers are already aware of the product and its basic characteristics. Therefore, overall consumption is not affected significantly by advertising specific brands.

Instead of increasing total consumption, the objective of advertisers is to create brand loyalty and to encourage consumers to switch to their brand. Thus, effective advertisers gain market share at the expense of others, who lose market share. They do not try to increase the total market for the product. An example can illustrate why they don't.

The total retail value of beer produced annually in the U.S. is about $50 billion. If a producer's advertising campaign increases its market share by one percent, its sales would increase by $500 million. However, if the total market for beer increased by one percent, a brand with a 10% share of the market would only experience a sales increase of $50 million.

Clearly, a producer has a great incentive to increase market share, but little incentive (or ability) to increase the total market. For this reason, advertisers focus their efforts on established consumers. They seek to strengthen the loyalty of their own consumers and induce other consumers to try their brand.

Young People and Commercials

Much has been made of the fact that many young people have greater recognition of some alcohol beverage brand labels than of former U.S. presidents. These reports make great press but what does it all mean? Probably not much because there is no evidence that such recognition leads to experimentation, consumption, or abuse. Sometimes it even appears to be related to less drinking later.

Similarly, most adults are probably much better at identifying photos of popular entertainers than of William Henry Harrison, Franklin Pierce, Chester Arthur, John Tyler, or other former presidents of the U.S. That probably doesn't mean much either

A widely reported "fact" is that by the age of 18, the typical young person will have seen 100,000 beer commercials. However, to see that many such commercials, it appears that a person would have to view television for about 161,290 hours or 18.4 years. Thus, a person would have to begin watching TV 24 hours a day, each and every day, from birth until after age 18.

In reality, viewers are much more likely to see alcohol portrayed during TV programs than during commercials. For example, an analysis of prime time TV found that alcohol commercials appeared at the rate of 0.2 per hour while drinking portrayals during programs occurred 25 times more frequently at five times per hour.

Perhaps those who want to reduce the presence of alcohol on television should propose eliminating the programming and let children watch commercials instead.

Overactive Imaginations

You haven't noticed them?! All those swirls, squiggles, and unusual shapes in ice cubes, on bottles, in liquid being poured, and elsewhere in alcohol beverage ads. The Center for Science in the Public Interest insists that "With little imagination, one can see some of these elements as faces, animals, breasts, penises, death masks, and other forms. . . ." This assertion may tell us more about the Center for Science in the Public Interest than about the ads.

Most people can easily imagine or "see" faces, animals, and other objects in clouds and inkblots, but the Center for Science in the Public Interest suggests that the "unidentified printed objects" in alcohol beverage print ads are intentionally placed there by advertisers, apparently to subconsciously seduce people to drink. Astonishingly, it actually calls for an investigation of these sinister objects, including having "corporate executives testify under oath on the witness stand." And while the Center for Science in the Public Interest is at it, perhaps it should call for a Congressional investigation of clouds and inkblots.

The Positive Side of Alcohol Advertising

One of the main arguments against alcohol beverage ads on television is that they "normalize" drinking in the minds of young viewers. To the extent that this is true, the ads may be performing a positive role.

The commonplace nature of alcohol ads on TV serves not to glamorize the products, as some critics suggest, but to cast them as mundane consumer products, right alongside aspirin, cookies, and alkaline batteries. That's a constructive way for young people to view them.

On the other hand, if we treat beverage alcohol as a dangerous substance to be avoided and not even advertised, we inadvertently raise it up from the ordinary into the realm of the powerful, the tantalizing, and the desirable Big Deal. In so doing, we slip into the familiar, failed pattern of demonizing the substance of alcohol rather than discouraging irresponsible behavior.

We should help young people regard the substance of alcohol as neutral—neither inherently good nor inherently bad. What matters is how it is used, and we must convey by word and example that the abuse of alcohol is never humorous, acceptable, or excusable.

Do alcohol ads portray the products being enjoyed in the most appealing settings and by the most attractive people? Of course they often do—no less than do ads for cars, instant coffee, and anti-fungal sprays. That normalcy of alcohol ads helps demystify the product—which is a good place to begin encouraging realistic, moderate, and responsible attitudes about it.

Responsible attitudes toward alcohol are based on the understanding that such beverages are yet another part of life over which individuals have control, like exercise, personal hygiene, or diet.

If alcohol beverages are to be used moderately by those who choose to consume them, then it's important that these beverages not be stigmatized, compared to illegal drugs, and associated with abuse. They aren't dangerous poisons to be hidden from sight and become a subject of mystery and perhaps fascinating appeal. But that would be the message sent if alcohol commercials were banned from TV.

Parental Influence

In spite of all the colorful rhetoric and emotional anecdotes, alcohol commercials do not cause young people to drink. The greatest influence of their beliefs, attitudes, and behaviors are from their parents.

Parents are much more influential than they generally realize. For example, among six things that might affect their decisions about drinking, 62% of American youth aged 12 to 17 identified their parents as a leading influence:

- Parents (62 percent)
- Best friends (28 percent)
- Teachers (9 percent)
- What they see on television (7 percent)
- What they see in ads (4 percent)

It is parents, rather than alcohol ads, with the great influence over young people.

CHAPTER 2

TEEN ALCOHOL ABUSE AND ITS EFFECTS

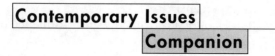

Contemporary Issues
Companion

THE DANGERS OF ALCOHOL

Kathiann M. Kowalski

In the following selection, Kathiann M. Kowalski explains how alcohol affects teenagers. She notes that alcohol consumption damages the liver, affects the brain, and can alter behavior. Consequently, teenagers who drink heavily often make unwise decisions, such as getting into violent fights or engaging in unprotected sexual intercourse. Kowalski also asserts that alcohol can destroy the relationships that teenagers have with their families and friends. Kowalski is a health writer for various magazines.

When a person takes a drink of alcohol, ethanol (the chemical name for drinkable alcohol) irritates the stomach lining, releasing acids. A small amount is broken down chemically, but most of the alcohol heads toward the small intestine through an opening called the pyloric valve. Drinking too much alcohol too quickly can cause the valve to swell and close, causing vomiting.

How Alcohol Affects the Body

From the small intestine, alcohol speeds into the bloodstream and toward the brain, where it depresses the central nervous system. By affecting the brain's production of chemicals called neurotransmitters, alcohol alters the person's behavior and the body's ability to function. Brain functions slow, decreasing balance, eyesight, and reasoning ability.

A "drink" is 12 ounces of beer or wine cooler, 4 ounces of wine, or 1 ounce of 86-proof whiskey. With one drink, a 160-pound adult male's blood alcohol level rises to 0.02 (2/10 of a gram of alcohol per 100 milliliters of blood). The drinker may feel relaxed and carefree.

Two and a half drinks in an hour shoots our 160-pound male's blood alcohol level up to 0.05. (The level is even higher for women, because they absorb more alcohol per drink into the bloodstream than men due to different enzyme levels in the stomach.) The drinker feels "high," and judgment is clearly affected. With alcohol blocking brain functions that restrain certain behaviors, the drinker may get loud and rowdy.

Shouting insults and taking offense at comments that normally would be shrugged off, drinkers can—and do—get into violent fights. Other drinkers wind up in riots like those that erupted [in September 1997] at the University of New Hampshire. Teens who would never otherwise break the law could find themselves jailed for joy riding in a stolen car, holding up a liquor store, or other crimes. Young people who typically act responsible sexually may expose themselves to unwanted pregnancies or even AIDS by engaging in unprotected intercourse.

At about 0.10 blood alcohol level, the drinker loses practically all judgment, dexterity, and coordination. Slurring words and staggering around the room, drinkers insist they are not drunk. At a blood alcohol level of 0.20, the drinker may explode in a violent rage, yet not even remember it later. Between 0.40 and 0.50, the person sinks into a coma.

When drinkers use other drugs, too, they run even more serious health risks. Consuming alcohol and depressant pills, for example, multiplies the effects—and the dangers—of each drug.

The Metabolic Process

Like sand flowing constantly through an hour glass, alcohol flows through the body until it is metabolized, or chemically broken down. No amount of coffee, exercise, or "chasers" can speed the process.

"First-pass metabolism" of part of the alcohol occurs in the stomach, and about 5 percent of the alcohol is released unchanged through sweat and breath. The greater portion of the alcohol, however, must be processed by the liver. Acetaldehyde dehydrogenase (ADH) converts ethanol to acetaldehyde. Acetaldehyde is further converted to acetic acid and then to carbon dioxide and water. The process takes about an hour per drink in a 160-pound adult male.

While this occurs, the liver can't function effectively in its normal job of converting stored fats and other nutrients into glucose, the sugar used by the body for energy. Over time, heavy drinkers can develop fatty deposits in the liver or suffer cirrhosis, a fatal disease involving scarring and hardening of the liver tissue.

Even after alcohol is metabolized, the body needs time to recover from the drug's onslaught. An all-too-common result is a hangover: throbbing headache, dull eyes, grogginess, and dehydration.

Alcohol Ruins Lives

Even if drinking doesn't lead to acute alcohol poisoning, teens can ruin their lives through chronic drinking. Over time, the body builds up a resistance to alcohol, craving more of the drug to get the same "high." Teens are more susceptible to developing addictions because they are still growing, both physically and emotionally. Approximately 3.3 million Americans ages 12 to 26 are problem drinkers.

Alcohol addiction can be devastating. A dramatic drop in grades and increased absenteeism can be the least of a young alcoholic's problems. Drunkenness can lead to violence, and other crimes, such as stealing and robbery, to pay for more alcohol.

Personal relationships dissolve into nothing. Tensions between teens and parents can go from bad to worse. Friendships disappear, until the only people around are those who also drink or use drugs.

Over time, alcohol wears away the body. If acute alcohol poisoning, violence, or an accident doesn't kill a chronic drinker, chances are increased risks of liver disease, heart disease, and cancer will.

TEENAGE ALCOHOL ABUSE CAN LEAD TO RISKY SEXUAL BEHAVIOR

Susan Foster

In the following selection, Susan Foster explains that teenagers who drink or use drugs are more likely to engage in risky sexual behavior, including having multiple partners and not using protection against pregnancy or sexually transmitted diseases. Foster cites a report released by the National Center on Addiction and Substance Abuse at Columbia University (CASA) that revealed that teenagers who use alcohol are as much as seven times more likely to have intercourse. She argues that parents can offset the dangerous decisions their children might make by becoming more involved in their lives. Foster is the vice president and director of policy research and analysis at CASA. The center studies the ways in which substance abuse affects society.

A PBS "Frontline" documentary chronicled an outbreak of syphilis among a large circle of teens in a suburban Atlanta community. What was even more alarming to health officials and the community was the revelation of a pattern of sex among upwards of 200 teens, focused around a group of girls, some as young as 13, with multiple partners, drinking and drug use, little if any protection, with no regard for the consequences.

The events in Georgia raise the question of whether this was an isolated incident or a harbinger of teen life around the country. What is certain is the disturbing connection between teen drinking and drug use and the increased likelihood of sexual activity.

A Troubling Report

A new report released [in December 1999] by The National Center on Addiction and Substance Abuse at Columbia University (CASA) raises troubling concerns about substance use and teen sexual activity: Teens who drink or use drugs are much more likely to have sex, initiate it at younger ages and have multiple partners, placing them at higher risk for sexually transmitted·diseases (STDs), AIDS and unplanned pregnancies.

Reprinted from Susan Foster, "Early Use of Booze, Drugs, Leads to Sex and Problems," *San Diego Union-Tribune*. Reprinted with permission from the author.

The report, "Dangerous Liaisons: Substance Abuse and Sex," is the result of a two-year, unprecedented analysis of the connection between drinking, drug use and sexual activity. The report's sobering conclusion finds that in America, drinking and drug abuse are bundled with high-risk sex.

Before graduating high school, and even as early as middle school—among 10- to 13-years-olds—every teen will have to make a conscious choice whether to drink or use illegal drugs and whether to have sex. Many teens will face all these decisions at once.

CASA's analysis shows that almost 80 percent of high school students have experimented with alcohol at least once. More than half had used at least one illicit drug. CASA's report noted the dramatic increase in just a generation of the proportion of 15-year-olds having sex: according to national surveys in 1970, less than 5 percent of 15-year-old girls and in 1972, 20 percent of 15-year-old boys, had engaged in sex. CASA's analysis reveals that in 1997, 38 percent of 15-year-old girls and 45 percent of 15-year-old boys have had sex.

The Link Between Alcohol and Sex

Among the report's key findings:

• Teens 14 and younger who use alcohol are twice as likely to have sex than those who don't.

• Teens 14 and younger who use drugs are four times likelier to have sex than those who don't.

• Teens 15 and older who drink are seven times likelier to have intercourse and twice as likely to have it with four or more partners than non-drinking teens.

• Teens 15 and older who use drugs are five times likelier to have sex and three times likelier to have it with four or more partners than those who don't.

Sixty-three percent of teens who use alcohol have had sex compared to 26 percent of those who never drank. Among teens who use drugs, 72 percent have had sex compared to 36 percent who have never used drugs.

Teens are more vulnerable to the combined lure of sex and alcohol and drugs. They are less able to cope with the potential consequences of drinking and using drugs which can undermine decisions about abstaining from sex, having unprotected sex and also trigger irresponsible and dangerous sexual behavior that can change the course of their lives.

The United States has the highest rate of STDs in the developed world. Teens are inconsistent condom users with or without alcohol and drugs which make the consequences of teen sexual activity linked to substance use clear: increased chances of infection by STDs such as syphilis, gonorrhea, chlamydia, as well as AIDS and unintended pregnancies.

What Parents Need to Do

While it is clear that teens who drink and use drugs are likelier to have sexual intercourse at earlier ages and with multiple partners, it is not clear which starts first—sexual intercourse or drinking or drug use. For parents, the point is that regardless of the sequence, either may be a red flag for the other. The report contains a loud and clear message for parents, clergy, school counselors and other caring adults: whichever teen activity—sex or substance use—first comes to their attention, these adults should be prepared to work with the teen on both matters.

Key to reducing a teen's risk of substance use is the power of parents. Parents have more influence over their children than they think. A CASA survey of 2,000 teens released in August 1999 showed that 42 percent of teens who don't use marijuana credit their parents over any other influence; teens who used marijuana say their friends are the primary influence in their decision to try the drug.

The same survey stressed the need for both parents to be engaged and involved in their children's lives. Children living in two-parent families who have a fair or poor relationship with their father are at 68 percent higher risk of smoking, drinking and using drugs compared to the average teen. Teens consistently rate moms more favorably than dads: more teens report having a very good or excellent relationship with their moms, say it's easier to talk to mom about drugs, credit mom more with their decision not to use marijuana, and go to her more often when confronted with major decisions.

The safest teens are those living with two parents and who have a positive relationship with both.

CASA's earlier teen survey also found that teens who attend a school where drugs are kept, used or sold are at twice the risk of substance abuse as teens attending a drug-free school. Schools can also do their part by creating comprehensive and age-appropriate education programs that address the association between substance abuse and sex.

When it comes to sex and substance abuse, how parents exercise their power in talking to their children about drinking, using drugs and engaging in sexual activity will be critical in how their children respond to the lure of alcohol, drugs and sex—as will the messages they send by their own behavior. For parents who believe that sexual abstinence before marriage is a moral imperative, the report signals the particular importance of persuading teens not to drink alcohol or use illegal drugs. For parents who consider teen sexual activity an inevitable or appropriate rite of passage, the CASA report points up the greater dangers for those teens who do drink and use drugs.

HOW TEEN ALCOHOLISM AFFECTED ONE FAMILY

Beth Kane-Davidson and Bill,
interviewed by Kathy Lowe Petersen

In the following selection, Kathy Lowe Petersen interviews Beth Kane-Davidson and Bill, the father of a young man, Ned, who became addicted to drugs and alcohol as a teenager. Bill explains the impact Ned's alcohol and drug addiction had on the family, noting that he was personally devastated by his son's initial refusal to respond to treatment. Bill and his wife turned to Al-Anon to help them cope with their feelings of guilt and co-dependency. Bill also describes the feelings of bewilderment and anger experienced by Ned's brother and grandparents. Kane-Davidson, the director of the Suburban Hospital Addiction Treatment Center in Bethesda, Maryland, offers advice for families in similar situations. Petersen is the president of the Lowe Family Foundation, an organization that helps families that are struggling to cope with alcohol abuse.

KATHY: Bill, can you briefly describe to us your family and how you found out about your son's problem with alcohol?

BILL: My wife, Jean, and I have been married for 28 years. We have two boys. Ned is the younger. Jean was a stay at home Mom until they were in the 5th & 6th grade. We were active in church, boy scouts, swim team, and PTA. For awhile we owned an airplane allowing us to travel extensively with the boys. We thought we were doing everything right.

In 1991, Ned was 14 years old and a very smart young boy. The first indication that there was a problem came when he got arrested for entering, with a key, a neighbor's house. He was put on probation and part of his probation was not to use drugs, even though there was no indication that he was doing drugs. A week or two after the arrest, I found a plastic bag in his bedroom and realized it was glue. This was the first indication I had of his use of substances. He told me that it was the first time he ever used it, didn't like it, and wouldn't do it

Excerpted from Beth Kane-Davidson and Bill, interviewed by Kathy Lowe Petersen, "May 1999 Interview with Beth Kane-Davidson on Teen Addiction and Recovery," available at www.lowefamily.org/interviews/may99.html. Reprinted with permission from the Lowe Family Foundation.

ever again. He told me how he had heard at school, as well as at home, how dangerous it was.

Later that summer, his rebellious nature started breaking out and the court suggested that he go see a psychiatrist. The psychiatrist only told us that he was a risk taker. We didn't understand what that meant and did not pursue it. We were very unfamiliar and uncomfortable with that whole process.

In the summer he went away to church camp and came home smoking. His clothing started to change and his music was changing to very heavy metal, which was very unusual, for our family listens to classical music. He started hanging around with low economic, low achieving kids. . . .

Ned's Experience in Treatment

KATHY: How old was he when he went into treatment? Was it a crisis situation?

BILL: He was 15. His behavior was just outrageous. He was very rebellious and screaming and yelling at us. He was saying things that didn't make any sense at all. He was running away for a day at a time. We were very concerned. He had total disregard for any authority—police, church, us, just a lot of outrageous behavior. We finally realized we needed help, so we started talking to people in November—close to 6 months after the arrest. Once we started talking to people who had children in trouble, we started realizing how similar their problems were to ours even though we had no evidence of drugs. Finally, a family that we knew told us about their son and it was almost an identical story. So, we started making a parallel comparison of their son to ours. It looked the same. By this time we were not afraid to talk about the problem. We saw so many parallels we decided that it must be substances even though we couldn't see it. Once he went into treatment, we discovered he was a significant abuser of alcohol, inhalants, and marijuana.

KATHY: How long was Ned in treatment?

BILL: He went into treatment in January 1992, for three weeks. They recommended that he go away for another 6-week program. He was at that program for eight weeks and then suddenly got well. He started doing everything right. He wanted to get out. He came home in April, but didn't want to go to school. He didn't want to go to the Phoenix School, which is a school for high-risk adolescents. The reason he didn't want to go there was that they wouldn't allow him to smoke. He didn't mind the school piece, but he wanted to smoke. And smoking was the priority. If he couldn't smoke, he wasn't going to school.

KATHY: So, he hadn't really dealt with his addiction?

BILL: I didn't think so.

BETH: Ned had had a temporary vacation from his addiction, but he obviously hadn't surrendered himself to his disease. That is the most difficult part. Anyone can do treatment. You can formulate and facilitate an intervention. You can get people into treatment. Sometimes you have to do it twice or three times, but eventually you can get someone in treatment. When someone is in treatment, it is fairly easy to follow the program. You have a lot of activity about recovery; you have people managing your life, doing things for you, and helping you get to where you have to go. But when you get out of treatment, boom, you are back in the real world.

The hardest thing I see for young adults to do is to let go of their old friends. So, generally, they are willing to do A, B, & C but not D. Similarly, Ned was not going to let go of his smoking. He was not going to let go of something that would keep him out of a school that was really geared toward his recovery. Recovery was not his number one priority. With adolescents we like to keep them in treatment with us for up to a year. Recovery is not an event; it is a process. It is a long, slow process—a day at a time, a minute at a time, and sometimes a second at a time.

And getting to that place where you are willing to say, "I am not going to let anything get in the way of my recovery," is truly remarkable. Forget smoking, friends, and school, for recovery is number one.

BILL: When he came home, I realized that he was not much different from when he left except he was not using. But I didn't even know he was using before he went in. It was absolutely devastating to me, to me personally. I was destroyed. When he came home, my world was ended. I could not function anymore. I had to do something for myself. It really hurt me a great deal.

When Ned came home, his social group was in fact now the people in AA. Of course, it was better than nothing. After a few months he relapsed. This time he had gone to the upper class. It was no more the low-life now; it was the very rich. He found people who gave him an abundance of very high-grade substances, both alcohol and drugs. He spent very little of his own money. He had very nice friends, and they gave him anything he wanted. He went into treatment the first time in handcuffs, and he went in the second time in handcuffs. But he was ready the second time to go. We sent him to a long-term program for nine and a half months. He then went to a halfway house for 14 months.

A Parental Response

KATHY: You said, Bill, that you were devastated. What kind of recovery did you and your wife work on?

BILL: Right after Ned went into treatment, someone told us to go to Al-Anon. I found it wonderful. The twelve-step program was very appealing to me. I was overrun by guilt, shame, and fear. I believed that I was personally responsible for Ned's being in trouble and I could not get past that. The twelve-step program offered me a chance to talk to others about that. Jean and I now at least had a language of recovery to talk about. We went on a family retreat and heard about the family aspect of addiction, co-dependency, enabling, and an introduction to Alcoholics Anonymous. I identified with that whole process. I saw how I had been living very much an alcoholic way of thinking, even though I wasn't drinking. The twelve-step program addressed my needs a great deal. I was still hurting very much.

KATHY: *Is that what parents should do, Beth?*

BETH: Yes, especially with an adolescent. It is very important to have the parents involved. At Suburban our push in treatment is for parents to have their own education about this disease. A part of having this disease is understanding what you have. The major goal in treatment for the adolescent is to become an expert. It doesn't do any good for me to know everything as the therapist. What will help is for me to make the patient the expert so he/she can look at it and say, "Aha, that's me." So we need to teach the parents what is enabling and what is provoking this behavior. Another thing to consider is that you have this young adult in treatment and now he is coming home. Now what? How is the house going to run? What are the rules? What are we going to do?

KATHY: *I would imagine that it is difficult for kids who are in treatment but also trying to cope with a parent's abuse or addiction of his/her own? Is that true, Beth?*

BETH: Yes, it is very difficult. We hear adolescents just in the basic level of prevention programs say to our trainers, "What do I do if I am at a restaurant with my Dad and he has three martinis and he wants me to get in the car with him?" It's a tough answer to give them. Some of these kids are going home after treatment to a family with parents drinking every night, and what do they do about it? It really does become a difficult job in having the whole family together and talking about the disease.

A survey of high school students states that over 50 per cent of parents have never spoken to their children about alcohol and drugs. Part of the push in education is really to get out there and talk to the parents about what they are doing at home and what is the message they are communicating to their children. Just as Bill was saying, what a shock when Ned first came home from treatment, here he has been away, and you are thinking everything is going to be back on track. But it doesn't happen. The family has changed.

Establishing Rules

BILL: One of the sad parts of Ned's experience was that, when he came home, he wasn't ready to recover yet. Jean and I had by then quite a bit of Al-Anon experience, and we were definitely not going to be taken down that path again. We had a very firm line that under no circumstances was he going to be using anything. We had a zero tolerance rule. I mean there was no smoking in the house; if there was any evidence of substance, we were going to stop him. We were not afraid of anything—the criminal justice system, doctors, were not afraid of him or the stigma. That made it tough for him. He had to go someplace else. The secrets were not in our house. He fell down hard quickly the second time because we were not going to enable him.

BETH: And that's what saved his life.

BILL: Yes. We weren't there to do anything but scrape him up and watch them put the handcuffs on him. When he went into treatment the second time, his first comment to me at 2 o'clock in the morning was, "I guess this means long term?" My reply was "No question about it."

BETH: You and Jean had been educated and empowered to do the exact thing that saved his life. The first stage of treatment for kids and for parents is basically, "Okay, no more secrets, no more denial, here are the facts. This is what it is. If it walks like a duck, quacks like a duck, it is a duck. This is where we are."

KATHY: *So you really have to be tough on this disease?*

BETH: You have to be kind and caring but firm. You can't be judgmental. You have to show concern. You need to know your goal. Often when people do interventions, they are not clear in what the goal is, so the intervention doesn't work. "My goal is to make everything better." "My goal is just to have this person stop drinking." Well, that's probably been the unspoken goal for the last 6–7 months (or years) of this person's addiction. The goal for the intervention is to get this person into appropriate treatment. It's being kind and caring but really knowing what you are doing. To many parents the word tough means, "I am going to be tough with you, so you better shape up or you are out." Maybe at some point that is the appropriate thing to do. But there are many steps before that step. It's better to say, "I am concerned for your health, your well being and our family. This is what I need you to do, and if you don't do this, these will be your options. I need you to go talk to a counselor and I will go with you. It's at 2 o'clock, it's in one hour. The car is outside and we are going to go.

The Effect on Other Relatives

KATHY: *How did the other family members react?*

BILL: My parents (68–72 years old at the time) were unfamiliar with the disease of alcoholism. They had no experience of it at all. They knew a few people who had been in AA. We had no experience with alcoholism in our family. My parents were bewildered, but very supportive. They did not know or understand it as a disease. They thought it was over-reactive to put him in a hospital. They didn't understand that. After a time they thought we were being too generous. They had a lot of black and white thinking, like me.

Ned's older brother had a great deal of resentment for the attention that Ned was receiving throughout this whole time. He knew more than we knew, and he thought we were too easy on him. While we were in the dark about what Ned was doing, he knew but did not tell us. He was very bitter and still is at the whole thing. Both boys were very angry with me. The one thought I was too easy; the other thought I was too hard. I was definitely the lightning rod.

Jean's family acted as though it never happened. They still believe it is a non-event. Fortunately, Jean and I both agreed 100 per cent that we were not going to allow this type of behavior in our family.

KATHY: Is alcoholism in your or your wife's family history?

BILL: My family's background is pretty stable. My parents drink very little, as do my two brothers. Jean's parents were married for about 35 years before her mother died. She is the oldest of seven children. Her father was an alcoholic but has been sober for 15 years. He stopped drinking because things got pretty bad in the family. Her paternal grandmother was probably an undiagnosed alcoholic. One of Jean's brothers died at 39 from complications of substance abuse and prescription drugs. Several of her siblings are currently abusing alcohol and/or substances.

KATHY: Did you and Jean realize that alcoholism was in her family?

BILL: Never occurred to me. Never heard such a thing. And I read extensively. It's interesting how denial works. There are whole areas of books that I read in which I would skip over the chapters dealing with addiction. We even had gone to a church series with John Bradshaw as a speaker, and we skipped the session on the dysfunctional family because it didn't apply to us. And this was when Ned was in the midst of his first crisis. We skipped anything that would have told us what we really needed to know.

KATHY: Beth, why do families do that?

BETH: Denial. We don't want it to be that. If I don't know, then I don't have to compare us to a sick family. Fortunately, families who stick with a family program finally get it and wake up. That is why so many treatment programs make it mandatory, while the adolescent is in treatment, that the family attend recovery sessions, too.

BILL: Even if they are kicking and screaming. . . .

BETH: Right, the total family. Unfortunately, I see all the time, when I go out to speak to parents at schools on prevention tips and education about alcohol and drugs, the parents are not there. The school really has to work hard to promote it to get the parents to come. It's sad when only 5 or 10 parents come. It's such an important subject. And so much needs to be taught to parents on how to talk to kids about alcohol and drugs. But, it's not on their priority list.

BILL: There is so much shame attached from the parent's point of view. "If I go to a public group and listen to someone talking about drug or alcohol abuse that must mean that I have a problem." That is the way of thinking. It's interesting that the people who need to be there don't go. The fear is that they might hear something they don't want to hear or be associated with the problem.

BETH: Also, parents are pulled into a trap that the kids set up for them. Which is, "You don't trust me?" You hear, "No other mother calls. No other mother does this. No other mother drops off her kid. You must not trust me." So, the parents start to back off. One of the most important things in the subject of alcohol and drug awareness is not to get trapped in the "You don't trust me" syndrome. It really should be, "I am your parent and I am going to parent you." Even to take it a step further, "I am going to network with your friend's parents, too.". . .

Do Not Permit Alcohol Consumption

KATHY: Bill, after living through this, what is your recommendation for parents of teens and preteens?

BILL: I firmly believe in *zero tolerance when it comes to drinking or drugs*. The idea that an occasional beer or a small glass of wine for a boy or girl at the age of 12, 14, or 16 is okay is totally wrong. One joint is one too many. Even the idea of a designated driver is wrong, for it gives the wrong message to young people. "Sure, son, go ahead and drink at a party; just get home safe." Being around young teens while they are drinking is dangerous and illegal. The other recommendation is for parents to reach out for help if they even think there may be a problem. Talking about the fear to another person helps everyone involved. Keeping the "secret" can be deadly for the child and can destroy a marriage and the whole family.

MANY TEENAGERS ARE NOT AWARE OF THE EFFECTS OF DRINKING ON PREGNANCY

David P. MacKinnon, Rhonda M. Williams-Avery, and Mary Ann Pentz

In the following article, David P. MacKinnon, Rhonda M. Williams-Avery, and Mary Ann Pentz detail the results of a study on teenagers' understanding of the cause and symptoms of fetal alcohol syndrome (FAS). According to the authors, while most teenagers are aware that alcohol consumption during pregnancy can harm the fetus, they have misconceptions about FAS and the risks of moderate drinking. The authors conclude that education is needed to increase the understanding of FAS. MacKinnon is a psychology professor at Arizona State University in Tempe, Arizona. Williams-Avery is a professor of psychiatry at the University of Washington in Seattle. Pentz is a professor in the Institute for Preventive Research at the University of Southern California's Keck School of Medicine.

Heavy maternal drinking during pregnancy has been associated with a pattern of craniofacial defects and abnormalities in growth, limb, and performance known as fetal alcohol syndrome (FAS). When babies with observable anatomic or functional problems less severe than FAS are born to mothers who have used alcohol during pregnancy, the term alcohol-related birth defects (ARBD) may be applied. FAS recently became the most common birth defect, outranking spina bifida and Down syndrome. The health and other costs of caring for FAS and ARBD babies and children are estimated at billions of dollars annually.

Because FAS and ARBD are entirely preventable by avoiding alcohol during pregnancy and because those afflicted with FAS and ARBD suffer lifelong difficulties, national efforts to increase awareness of FAS and ARBD have become a high priority. Despite these efforts, recent surveys suggest that alcohol consumption during pregnancy continues.

Although knowledge of the risks of drinking while pregnant is very

Excerpted from David P. MacKinnon, Rhonda M. Williams-Avery, and Mary Ann Pentz, "Youth Beliefs and Knowledge About the Risks of Drinking While Pregnant," *Public Health Reports*, November/December 1995.

high among adults in both national and local surveys such as the National Health Interview Survey, a telephone survey of U.S. adults, adults in Multnomah County, Oregon, and recently pregnant women in Los Angeles County, there are considerable misconceptions about fetal alcohol syndrome and the risk of moderate drinking. To the best of our knowledge, no studies have addressed whether these beliefs are also present among young persons.

In this selection, our purpose is to describe the beliefs and knowledge about the risks of drinking during pregnancy in several large samples of young persons. Youth are an important population to study because during these years, experimentation with alcohol begins, and many attitudes regarding alcohol are established. The high prevalence of teenage pregnancy also makes research on awareness of alcohol's effects on the fetus important in this age group. Our questions were patterned after those in other studies to compare between youth and adult beliefs about drinking while pregnant. We also examine beliefs about the risk of drinking while pregnant by sex, ethnicity, alcohol use, and grade in school. . . .

Survey Results

Of approximately 27,544 students who were asked, "Can drinking alcohol while pregnant cause birth defects?" 81 percent responded "Yes, definitely." When both the "Yes, Definitely," and "Yes, Probably" response options are combined, 97 percent responded affirmatively to this question. . . . In every sample, males were less likely to perceive maternal prenatal drinking as a risk to the fetus than females. Older students were more likely to respond that drinking during pregnancy was a risk to the fetus. Ethnicity and socioeconomic status were not associated substantially with the perception of risk of maternal drinking during pregnancy. . . .

Awareness of FAS and knowledge about FAS and appropriate alcohol use were measured for 3,478 students in the Indianapolis 1991–92 sample and all 1,084 in the college sample. . . . Seventy-two percent of the 4,173 students in the college and Indianapolis samples asked whether or not they had heard of FAS responded yes. The main sources of this awareness were school magazines and television (36 percent). Of the high school students, 47.8 percent thought that FAS was a baby born addicted to alcohol, 5.3 percent thought that it was a baby born drunk, while 46.9 percent correctly thought that FAS described a baby born with certain birth defects. Ninety-five percent of the sample correctly believed that FAS could be prevented. However, 50.3 percent of the sample also incorrectly believed that FAS could be cured, and 48.5 percent believed it could be inherited.

More than 96 percent of the total sample that answered FAS knowledge questions believed that FAS was caused by a woman drinking too much during her pregnancy. Knowledge about the definition of too much was inconsistent, however. Approximately 78.8 percent of the high school sample and 62.1 percent of the college sample thought that all alcohol during pregnancy should be avoided, and 3.4 percent of the high school sample and 1.9 percent of the college sample reported that a pregnant woman could have at least three–four glasses of alcohol per week.

Twenty-five percent of the high school students and 13.7 percent of the college students felt that it was acceptable for a pregnant woman to consume four–five alcoholic drinks on one occasion during the pregnancy. Eighty-six percent of the students felt that it was extremely beneficial for a woman to avoid all alcohol during pregnancy. Those students least likely to believe in total abstinence during pregnancy were younger males and those who had been drunk in the last 30 days.

A composite of FAS knowledge, consisting of the number of correct responses to the following questions: "Have you heard of FAS?" (yes was treated as a correct response), "Which best describes FAS?" "Can FAS be prevented?" "Can FAS be cured?" "Can FAS be inherited?" "Is FAS caused by a woman drinking too much during her pregnancy?" and "Are children with severe FAS physically and mentally retarded?" was correlated with five demographic and alcohol use variables separately in the Indiana and Arizona college student samples. Among high school students, FAS knowledge was significantly related to sex, grade, and the number of times the subject was drunk in the last month. Only white ethnicity was related to knowledge in the college sample and only when adjusted for the other predictors.

A second composite variable measuring beliefs about abstinence during pregnancy was based on four questions: "How beneficial is it for pregnant women to avoid all alcohol?" "Does a mother's occasional use of alcohol while pregnant place her baby at risk for birth defects?" "Is it OK for a pregnant woman to have four–five alcoholic drinks at one time during her pregnancy?" and "How many drinks is it OK for a pregnant woman to have?" Males, younger respondents, and persons who consumed alcohol were less likely to endorse abstinence during pregnancy.

Some Understanding of Fetal Alcohol Syndrome

Most of the respondents surveyed believe that drinking while pregnant is potentially harmful to the fetus, that avoiding all alcohol during pregnancy is extremely beneficial, and that FAS can be prevented. Younger persons and males are less likely to believe that drinking alcohol while pregnant is harmful and that pregnant women should abstain completely. Although many young people are aware of the risks of drinking while pregnant, many endorse a safe level of drinking that is higher than the Surgeon General's abstinence recommendation.

There are also misconceptions about the exact meaning of fetal alcohol syndrome, as found among adults studied by others. More than a quarter of students at both the high school and college level have not heard of fetal alcohol syndrome. Of those who have heard of FAS, less than half know what FAS is; almost half incorrectly believe that FAS describes a baby born addicted to alcohol or a drunk baby. Moreover, 50.3 percent of the high school students and 39.1 percent of the college students believe that FAS can be cured. Prior studies of adults differ in age and sample selection, making direct comparisons with the present sample difficult. Despite these differences, the conclusions from this sample of young persons are similar to earlier studies of adults. Most respondents believe that pregnant women should abstain from using alcohol. Although this general belief among youth (81 percent for our beliefs question) is similar to adult samples, for example, 84 percent for ages 18–44, the youth sample had more accurate knowledge of specific consequences of alcohol use. The 1985 National Health Interview Survey sampled nearly 20,000 adult respondents, ages 18–44. Only 55 percent of that sample had ever heard of FAS, and of those who had, only 24 percent correctly identified FAS. In our study, 73 percent of high school students and 70 percent of college students had heard of FAS, and approximately 47 percent of the high school students and 45 percent of the college students correctly identified FAS as a baby born with certain birth defects.

Minor and Van Dort also found in 1982 that awareness of FAS was low. Of their sample of recently pregnant women, only 55 percent had heard of FAS. However, of this subsample, 80–97 percent were in agreement with current expert knowledge about FAS on four questions (Can FAS be inherited, prevented, caused by a woman drinking too much during pregnancy, and characterized by mental and physical retardation?), with the exception being that 50 percent thought that FAS could be cured. Although more students in our samples had heard of FAS, slightly fewer were accurate in their beliefs about the syndrome: 54 percent, 97 percent, 86 percent, and 82 percent answered the aforementioned questions correctly, and 48 percent thought that FAS could be cured.

Given the association between alcohol use and FAS and ARBD, the lack of conclusive research describing the risky level of moderate drinking and the difficulty of diagnosing FAS and ARBD at birth, abstinence from alcohol during pregnancy remains the most prudent message for prevention strategies among adolescents. Specific knowledge deficits and inaccurate beliefs may lead to uncertainty about the safety of alcohol consumption and the severity of FAS. Of particular concern are those adolescents who use alcohol and get drunk regularly, whose beliefs about abstinence during pregnancy are the least conservative. Knowledge of FAS and beliefs about abstinence are positively correlated, suggesting that increasing FAS knowledge may be associated with increased beliefs about abstaining from alcohol during pregnancy.

How to Teach Teenagers About Fetal Alcohol Syndrome

Education to increase knowledge of FAS among young persons might be best delivered jointly through schools and mass media. When asked where they had heard about FAS, both college and high school students most commonly reported "school," followed by "magazines" and "television." Warnings on alcohol beverages, posters in establishments that sell alcohol, and warnings on alcohol advertisements may increase awareness, but existing warning posters and labels do not specifically mention FAS and ARBD. Strategies to increase awareness in schools should be delivered in a way so that the preventive effects on other alcohol-related problems such as drinking and driving and violence are not reduced.

On the other hand, the consensus about the harm of alcohol consumption while pregnant may enhance social norm manipulations. Increased knowledge and awareness of the risk of drinking while pregnant may ultimately alter societal norms regarding maternal alcohol use.

Mothers of FAS and ARBD babies have been characterized by more chronic and severe alcohol-related problems than women who discontinue alcohol use during pregnancy. More intensive and focused prevention efforts are likely required with this group. The effects of treatment programs for such pregnant addicted women and programs to increase knowledge and awareness of FAS and ARBD among health providers might be enhanced if programs were implemented in conjunction with more widely disseminated prevention efforts targeting the general public's awareness of the risks of a pregnant woman's alcohol consumption.

Youth appears to be an important group to target because of teenage pregnancy and the incomplete knowledge about the risk of drinking while pregnant. A rationale for this approach is that increasing knowledge of FAS among youth should occur before pregnancy because alcohol consumption can be problematic even in the earliest stages of pregnancy, and FAS information delivered to the general public may disseminate to persons at high risk for FAS. Care should be taken so that new strategies to prevent FAS do not reduce or dilute campaigns to prevent other alcohol-related problems such as drinking and driving.

Teenage Drinking Can Lead to Automobile Accidents

National Clearinghouse for Alcohol and Drug Information

In the following selection, the National Clearinghouse for Alcohol and Drug Information reports that alcohol consumption by teenagers leads to automobile accidents. According to the NCADI, more than 2,300 youth died in alcohol-related crashes in 1996. Young drivers have a higher rate of fatal alcohol-related automobile accidents than older drivers, the clearinghouse notes. However, the NCADI argues, these accidents can be prevented or reduced by the enforcement of zero tolerance and age 21 laws. NCADI is the information service of the Center for Substance Abuse Prevention of the Substance Abuse and Mental Health Services Administration in the U.S. Department of Health and Human Services.

Impaired driving is a preventable social problem that costs Americans billions of dollars each year. In 1996, more than 21 percent of drivers between 15 and 20 years of age involved in fatal crashes had blood alcohol concentrations (BACs) between 0.01 and 0.10. Examining trends in impaired driving provides answers to many questions concerning the nature and extent of this problem, such as who drives impaired and how impaired driving rates vary over time and by State. The following question-and-answer format presents the latest data in the field and summarizes the most effective strategies for preventing impaired driving by young people in the United States.

The Costs of Impaired Driving

How is impaired driving defined?

Impaired driving is the joint occurrence of (1) driving a vehicle and (2) having a BAC of 0.01 or greater or being under the influence of some other psychoactive substance. The National Highway Traffic Safety Administration (NHTSA) defines a fatal crash as "alcohol-related" if either a driver or a nonoccupant (e.g., pedestrian) has a BAC greater than or equal to 0.01 in a police-reported traffic crash.

Excerpted from National Clearinghouse for Alcohol and Drug Information, "Technical Report: Impaired Driving Among Youth: Trends and Tools for Prevention," available at www.health.org/pubs/qdocs/CSAP3P19.htm.

Those with a BAC of 0.10 or greater are considered "intoxicated." Separately, either driving or drinking may be socially acceptable and legal. However, combined they spell serious trouble. It is unlawful in all States for any person who is under the influence of any alcoholic beverage or any drug to drive a vehicle.

What is the magnitude of the problems caused by impaired driving?

The personal and societal costs associated with impaired driving are staggering. During 1996, alcohol-related motor vehicle crashes in the United States caused more than 17,000 deaths and more than 321,000 injuries. In 1996, alcohol-related fatalities for youth ages 15 to 20 increased by nearly 5 percent. More than 2,300 youth died in alcohol-related crashes (36.6 percent of their total traffic fatalities). Moreover, NHTSA reported that high BACs (in excess of 0.10 percent) accounted for all of the increase in alcohol-related fatalities among youth in 1996. The annual cost of alcohol-related crashes has been estimated at $148 billion. Though studied much less, it is likely that driver impairment from drugs adds to these costs. The groups most affected are teenagers and young adults. . . .

The lowest rates [of alcohol-related fatalities] are found in the northeastern States, such as New York (0.29 deaths per 10,000 population in 1996), Massachusetts (0.30 deaths), and Rhode Island (0.33 deaths). Rates three, four, and five times higher, respectively, are found in the South, Southwest, and Mountain States (but not Utah). In 1996, the States with the highest rates were New Mexico (1.41 deaths), Mississippi (1.24), Wyoming (1.20), and Alabama (1.14). . . .

Why are there such significant differences among States' rates?

A variety of factors interact to influence the rate of alcohol-related motor vehicle fatalities. These factors include population density, population composition (regarding age and sex), cultural differences, law enforcement techniques, and the like. States with large populations of young drivers and lenient drinking and driving policies are likely to have higher rates of alcohol-related motor vehicle fatalities. States that implement the effective strategies outlined later in this publication, such as increased enforcement of minimum purchase age laws, zero tolerance laws, and graduated licensing, are likely to see their death rates decline.

How do we know that driving under the influence of alcohol causes crashes?

The largest case-control study of drinking and driving ever conducted was completed in Grand Rapids, Michigan, during the early 1960's. The results for the 13,485 crash-involved and comparison drivers studied indicated that the risk of becoming involved in a crash increased after just a few drinks and increased exponentially with the number of drinks consumed. . . .

Crash risk increases gradually up to a BAC of about 0.10 percent (about four to five drinks in 1 to 2 hours for a 160-pound person). Then, crash risk increases exponentially with increasing amounts of alcohol. When compared with drivers who had not been drinking, drivers with BACs from 0.10 percent to 0.25 percent were 6 to 32 times more likely to become involved in a crash.

A Variety of Strategies

Are there any proven strategies for reducing impaired driving?

Yes. Research and evaluation efforts conducted in the late 1960's and 1970's suggested that crash reduction could be achieved by well-publicized, intensive law enforcement efforts. A prevention model emerged that suggested that reductions in alcohol-related crashes could be achieved by deterring potential offenders from drinking and driving. Such general deterrence involved creating a plausible risk of being apprehended, followed by the perception of certain and swift application of significant sanctions. In other words, the most effective approaches involved creating the perception among drivers that they would be well advised not to attempt driving after drinking.

Have these strategies been implemented?

The 1980's can be characterized as a decade of implementation for this general deterrence model. States began to enact laws to mandate license suspension and eliminate or restrict plea bargaining.

Many States made it illegal per se to drive with a specified BAC, typically 0.10 percent. Formerly, in order to be charged with impaired driving, a person had to display obvious signs of intoxication, and the BAC was considered only a contributory factor. Another innovation was administrative license revocation (ALR), which allowed confiscation of the driver's license at the time of arrest rather than at some future court date. States also began to introduce new sanctions to broaden penalties and treatments. Some were responsive to victims' rights (e.g., restitution), some were alternatives or adjuncts to jail sentences (e.g., community service and house arrest), and others were attempts to deal specifically with repeated drinking and driving behavior (e.g., ignition interlocks, vehicle confiscation, or registration withdrawal).

The 1990's have seen even stronger legislation, more numerous sobriety checkpoints, and an increasing interest in drugs other than alcohol. Additional States passed ALR, and some States have lowered their per se alcohol limit to 0.08 percent BAC. A favorable Supreme Court ruling in 1990 and several positive evaluation studies led to stronger support for sobriety checkpoints as a method of enforcing impaired-driving laws. Also, based on programs begun in Los Angeles during the 1980's, more than 4,000 police officers in 25 States were trained as drug recognition experts to provide them with the expertise to enforce impaired-driving laws in situations where the impairment was caused by drugs other than alcohol.

What special attention have underage drinking drivers received?

Drinking and driving by youth has been a major focus of preventionists for most of the past 15 years. In 1984, President Reagan signed legislation to withhold highway safety funds from States that did not set 21 as the minimum purchasing age for alcohol. By July 1988, all 50 States had set that minimum purchasing age. It is estimated that these laws have saved approximately 16,500 lives since [1985]. Many States also adopted low or zero tolerance presumptive BAC limits for drivers under the age of 21 and "use and lose" laws, which link drug and alcohol convictions, irrespective of motor vehicle involvement, to loss of the driver's license. . . .

Are crashes being prevented?

Yes. The numbers of vehicles, drivers, road miles, and miles driven have increased steadily throughout the 1980's and 1990's. Yet the numbers of alcohol-related fatalities, drinking drivers involved in fatal crashes, and drinking drivers randomly sampled in roadside surveys have declined.

In 1983, there were 23,646 alcohol-related fatalities in motor vehicle crashes (or 55 percent of all motor vehicle fatalities during that year). In 1996, there were 17,126 alcohol-related fatalities in motor vehicle crashes (or 41 percent of all motor vehicle fatalities in that year). Thus, for the period 1982 through 1995, both the absolute number of alcohol-related fatalities and the percentage of alcohol-related fatalities among all motor vehicle fatalities declined.

A similar method of assessing the decline in fatal crashes is to examine the BACs of drivers involved in these crashes. In 1982, approximately 9 percent of all drivers involved in fatal crashes had BACs between 0.01 percent and 0.09 percent at the time of the crash, and 30 percent had BACs of 0.10 percent or higher. By 1996, these percentages had declined to 6 percent and 19 percent, respectively.

Data from national roadside surveys conducted in 1973, 1986, and 1996 corroborate the declines in the fatal crash rates. Each of these surveys was conducted on weekend nights and involved voluntary breath tests of approximately 3,000 to 6,000 drivers sampled from around the country. . . . Approximately 5.1 percent of drivers sampled in 1973 had a BAC of 0.10 percent or higher. This figure dropped to 3.2 percent in 1986 and 2.8 percent in 1996. Steady declines were seen among all groups . . . except females, Hispanics, and adults aged 21–34. Research on female impaired drivers is fairly limited but suggests that females are drinking and driving more. For example, analyses . . . showed that when crash involvement for young females is examined, their alcohol-related deaths may actually be increasing. The increase seen among Hispanic drivers is of great concern in States with large Hispanic populations, and it warrants further attention. Declines were greatest among young drivers—possibly because of the minimum age 21 drinking laws promoted during the mid-1980's and the more recent zero tolerance or low BAC laws for youth.

Characteristics of Drivers and Victims

Who is still drinking and driving?

Despite progress, many people, especially males under age 25, continue to drink and drive. In 1996, 21 percent of all male drivers involved in fatal crashes had a BAC of 0.10 percent or greater, compared with only 11 percent of all female drivers involved in fatal crashes.

Most drinking drivers of passenger vehicles (including light trucks and vans) who were involved in fatal crashes were 25 to 34, followed by drivers under the age of 25, followed by those ages 35 to 44. Overall, the median driver's age was 31. When looking only at drivers whose BAC was between 0.01 percent and 0.09 percent, the age group with the highest rate of impaired drivers was under 25 years. Young drivers (15 to 20 years old) have a higher rate of fatal alcohol-related motor vehicle crashes than older drivers (per 100,000 population). A recurring finding in impaired-driving research has been that young drivers more frequently crash at lower BACs than do older drivers, perhaps because of the former's inexperience with drinking, with driving, or both.

Who is being killed in alcohol-related crashes?

In 1996, most of the 17,126 fatalities in alcohol-related crashes were drivers (10,135 or 60 percent), most of whom were between ages 16 and 44 (7,786 or 47 percent). The remainder were passengers (4,010 or 22 percent), pedestrians (2,599 or 15 percent), and others, including bicyclists (382 or 2 percent). Many of the passengers were children or teenagers (481 fatally injured passengers age 15 and younger, 789 between the ages of 16 and 20). The fatally injured pedestrians in alcohol-related crashes tended to be older (median age 39) than either the fatally injured drivers (median age 33) or the fatally injured passengers (median age 24).

The rate of alcohol-related fatal crashes per 100,000 population was highest during 1996 for persons ages 21 to 24, followed closely by the age groups 16 to 20 and 25 to 34. . . . While some children age 15 or younger and some persons age 65 or older die in these crashes, it is teenagers and young adults, followed by middle-aged adults, who suffer by far the greatest losses.

Do race and ethnicity make a difference?

Little is known about the race and ethnicity of fatally injured drivers and passengers in alcohol-related crashes. . . . A literature search on ethnic/racial group involvement in impaired driving found that African Americans and Hispanics are disproportionately more likely to be impaired drivers, but the relationship appeared to be reduced for ethnic/racial youth. The roadside survey data previously cited indicated that Hispanic drivers were more likely to have been drinking than Whites, Asians, or African Americans. Black adults ages 25 or older, Hispanic males, and Native Americans were more likely to have been drinking prior to their fatal crashes in which pedestrians were killed. Young Blacks, Hispanic females, and Asians were less likely to have been drinking.

Additional Factors

When do alcohol-related crashes occur?

The month with the largest number of alcohol-related motor vehicle deaths during 1996 was August (9.7 percent of 17,126 deaths). June was second (9.3 percent), followed by September (9.0 percent), November (8.8 percent), and October (8.6 percent). December ranked seventh (8.3 percent). The months with the fewest deaths were January (6.8 percent) and February (6.8 percent).

Consistent with popular belief, most deaths that resulted from alcohol-related crashes occurred on a Saturday (24 percent), followed by Sunday (20 percent) and Friday (16 percent). The day with the fewest alcohol-related crash deaths was Tuesday (9 percent).

The results for time of day confirm that most alcohol-related deaths resulted from crashes at night. The time of the crash for approximately two of every three alcohol-related deaths was between 8 P.M. and 5:59 A.M. (65 percent). Approximately 1 in 5 deaths occurred between 4 P.M. and 7:59 P.M. (20 percent), and approximately 1 in 10 occurred between 11 A.M. and 3:59 P.M. (9 percent).

Are drugs a problem?

No drug has been studied as extensively as alcohol has been studied with respect to motor vehicle crashes. Available evidence concerning drugs suggests that they have a small, yet measurable, association with impaired driving and the occurrence of impaired driving crashes. . . .

What works to prevent impaired driving among youth?

Overall, impaired driving has declined nearly every year since 1982. The reasons for the decline likely have involved the interaction of several factors, including the general deterrents described above, changing social attitudes fostered by citizen pressure, and generally lower levels of alcohol consumption. In 1996, however, alcohol-related fatalities for youth ages 15 to 20 increased by almost 5 percent. Much more progress needs to be made to prevent the more than 17,000 alcohol-related motor vehicle fatalities and 321,000 injuries that occur each year.

Many proven strategies can prevent these crashes or reduce their numbers, including those designed to enhance deterrence and those designed to affect alcohol consumption. Community organization and mobilization are often the mechanisms for implementing needed changes. [Here are] three of the many youth-oriented deterrence and alcohol policy strategies that have been shown to be effective.

Age 21 Laws Minimum age 21 alcohol purchase laws are now in place in all 50 States and the District of Columbia. NHTSA estimates that more than 16,500 traffic deaths have been averted since States started raising the minimum legal drinking age. Current laws are not well enforced, however. A number of strategies have been developed to improve enforcement and decrease youth access to alcohol. See, for example, the Center for Substance Abuse Prevention's (CSAP's) Teen Drinking Prevention Program materials.

Zero Tolerance Many States have enacted BAC limits of 0.02 percent or less for drivers under age 21. These limits reflect the facts that drinking is illegal for anyone under 21 and that young drivers are particularly vulnerable to impairment at low BACs. These laws have been found to reduce alcohol-related crashes in the affected age group by as much as 50 percent in some States and by between 17 and 22 percent consistently.

Graduated Licensing Graduated licensing is a process by which learning drivers can be gradually introduced to driving. Reductions in traffic crashes, both alcohol-related and non-alcohol-related, have been measured as a result of nighttime driving curfews, increased age of licensure, and graduated driving privileges in which a variety of driving restrictions are gradually lifted as the driver gains experience and maturity. Such licensing systems have been found to be very effective in New Zealand and Australia.

Impaired driving among youth is one negative consequence of the abuse of alcohol and other drugs, but it can be prevented. Implementing the three strategies—and other effective prevention strategies—can help communities and States in their efforts to decrease the personal and societal costs of crashes caused by young impaired drivers.

CHAPTER 3

PERSPECTIVES ON TEEN ALCOHOLISM

Sober Since Seventeen

Jan P.

In the following selection, Jan P. recounts her experiences as a teenage alcoholic. She explains that she began drinking and using drugs as a junior in high school, stopping when she became pregnant during her senior year. Jan writes that she decided to stay sober after giving birth for the sake of herself and her child. According to Jan, Alcoholics Anonymous, the church, and her family have helped her stay sober for fifteen years.

When people find out that I got sober at 17 and have been continuously sober for 15 years, they can hardly believe it. Some people even wonder how a 17-year-old girl could possibly have the kind of alcohol or drug problem that would require sobriety. Well, let me tell you . . . lots do.

The Beginning of an Addiction

I got high for the first time when I was 13. It was innocent enough; a friend came by the house with a joint and some beer, and we did it. For me, it was instant love. I had never felt that good in my life. After that, I got high whenever I had the chance. It was as simple as that. By the time I was 17, getting high was the most important thing in my life.

The funny thing is, I had a pretty good life. My parents were divorced, and I seldom saw my father, but I had a decent relationship with my mother. I had just about everything I wanted—a car, nice clothes, spending money, etc. I even had a boyfriend. So I don't think I was hiding from anything; I just loved the feeling of being high.

During my junior year in high school, I smoked pot on the way to school every morning and during lunch every day. I smoked pot and drank alcohol—at least a little bit—almost every night. Every once in a while, I scored coke, speed, or ecstasy.

One night, a guy had some coke, and he said he would share it with me if I would get naked with him. I said, "Why not?" After we did the coke, we had sex. It was so easy, and I didn't feel guilty or remorseful or anything. Before I knew it, I was sleeping with guys for drugs and money. I did not feel like a whore. I just thought of it as the barter system.

Facing a Pregnancy

I turned up pregnant about a month into my senior year. I planned to get an abortion, but I kept putting it off until it was too late. I talked to a counselor at an adoption agency. She convinced me to quit using alcohol and drugs until the baby was born. She didn't put any pressure on me to do anything else.

I told my mom about my situation when I was five months pregnant. To my surprise, she didn't freak. In fact, once she quit crying and blaming herself for being a bad mother, she said that she would support me in whatever decision I made. That was the first time that the idea of keeping and raising the baby crossed my mind. At eight months, I decided to do that.

I gave birth to Nikki on August 11, 1985. She was beautiful and healthy. My mom and my friends rallied around me. They all came to the hospital to see me and the baby. I felt happy. And one of the reasons I felt happy was because I knew that I could start getting high again. I decided not to breast feed for that reason. When we got home from the hospital, though, I put off getting high for a few days, even though pot and alcohol were both available. I remember thinking that we needed to get settled before I started using again. At first, I gave myself a couple of days. Then it stretched into a week. Then two.

I ventured out on my own for the first time when Nikki was 18 days old. I went over to visit a friend who I knew beyond any doubt would have some good smoke. Sure enough, after just a few minutes of chit chat, she rolled one and fired it up. I hesitated for a moment, but it was only a moment. I think I got stoned on the first hit. As before, I loved it. We spent the rest of the afternoon laughing and talking over beer and weed. I was flying high. I almost forgot about Nikki.

I got home about 10:00 P.M. My mom was furious, and she let me have it. For the first time in my life, I cursed at her and told her to shut up. I stormed off to my room, and when I slammed the door Nikki woke up and started crying. I picked her up and tried to comfort her, but it didn't feel right. It's like, I couldn't hold her right. I couldn't connect with her like I normally could. I didn't have that warm, sweet feeling for her that I had grown to love. I don't know how to explain it other than to say that it just didn't feel right.

At first I felt angry and impatient. Then I started crying. I called my mom. She came in and took Nikki, and as soon as she did, Nikki quit fussing and went back to sleep.

A Turning Point

Mom sat down beside me on my bed and put her arms around me. That's when I *really* cried. Then we talked. We talked for three solid hours. It was the first time we had ever talked like that or connected in that way. I was surprised to learn that she knew a lot more about me than I ever would have guessed. She knew about my drinking and pot smoking, though not to its full extent. She said that she had never confronted me about it because she lacked the strength and confidence in herself to do that. She had, however, studied up on teenage drinking and drug use, and she knew a lot about it.

I asked her what she thought I should do. She said that she thought I should do one of two things: Either give Nikki up for adoption and play out my wild streak, or keep her and become a responsible parent. And the latter choice had no place for alcohol and drugs. I knew immediately that she was right, and to my surprise, it was an easy choice. I chose Nikki. I thank God for that decision.

I reluctantly agreed to check out Alcoholics Anonymous (AA). I attended a few meetings, and although I did not like it, I remained willing to go if that was the only way to stay sober. Then I talked to an assistant pastor at my mom's church. He knew about AA, and we talked about AA's spirituality compared to the church's religion. He suggested that I give the church a whirl, either in addition to AA or in place of it. I chose the latter. And it turned out to be a good choice for me.

I didn't immerse myself in the church, but I did get involved. I joined a couple of groups—one for young adults and another for mothers, and I did some volunteer work. My faith in God grew stronger. I met some terrific people, both young and older, none of whom used drugs, and only a few of whom drank alcohol. I started dating again. I got a part-time job. I studied for and passed the high school equivalency exam. Then I attended trade school, got a real job, and saved some money. My faith in God continued to grow.

Just after Nikki turned four, she and I moved out of Mom's house and into our own apartment. I was 22 years old. I was a responsible parent. I was a good mother.

Through all of these life changes, I relied on God and the church for guidance and support. When I got scared, I prayed and talked to trustworthy people. When I thought about getting high, I prayed and talked to the assistant pastor who had brought me into the church. When I felt depressed or lonely, I increased my involvement in volunteer work.

The Benefits of Church and Alcoholics Anonymous

About a year after Nikki and I struck out on our own, I met a wonderful man on a church retreat. He was 27 and had been sober in AA for two years. We married one year later. He showed me AA in a different light than I had seen it at age 18. I gradually became "a member" of AA. I took my first AA sobriety chip on August 30, 1989, the fifth anniversary of the day that I made the decision, sitting on the edge of my bed with my mom, to be a responsible parent instead of a teenage alcoholic and drug addict.

So now I'm 32. Nikki is 14. She has grown up with two sober parents who love her dearly. To my knowledge, she does not use alcohol or drugs. My husband and I still attend AA. All three of us are very involved in the church. I truly love my life. I thank God every day for my exceedingly good fortune, which I call faith.

For me, AA and the church combine beautifully to give me the support I need for sobriety and for spiritual growth and change. I have heard other sober people say that they find the church incompatible with and unsupportive of AA. I have found just the opposite. A friend of mine summed it up nicely just the other day when he smiled and said, "Well, I guess Truth is Truth, regardless of where you hear it."

I STARTED DRINKING AS A TEENAGER

Brian

Brian describes how he began drinking as a teenager and how alcohol led to increasing problems into adulthood. According to Brian, he began drinking with friends in junior high. As his drinking persisted, Brian writes, his grades became progressively worse and he became less involved with school activities. When his drinking continued into adulthood, Brian notes that he became depressed and wanted to die. He explains how attending Alcoholics Anonymous helped end his dependence on alcohol.

I was born and raised in a very strict Irish-American family. I have never received a [driving-while-intoxicated conviction] (DWI), and on only one occasion drove a car under the influence of alcohol. I have never lost a job or a marriage and always had plenty of friends and drinking buddies. I was not on the Bowery and did not look even close to it. This is what my denial told me. I rationalized the problems in my life as being either my father's, my girlfriend's, or my boss's fault. I looked at people in Alcoholics Anonymous (AA) and thought that maybe if I was older or was as bad as they were I would stop. I said "easy for you to say, stop drinking. But I'm only 22."

Drinking in High School

When I was in grade school I was an altar boy and a boy scout. I received an award from the district attorney for citizenship and was generally very "uncool." When I started drinking I soon found a group of kids my age to party with. We did a lot of experimenting and had some fun. In the beginning of high school I began to drink more frequently, at least every weekend. I immediately got a part-time job to pay for my fun. I decided I never wanted my drinking money to be at anyone else's discretion, and I have never been unemployed since.

Suddenly, after a lot of drinking and some fun I was "cool." By my senior year I had very cute girlfriends, and I went to lots of parties and rock concerts. In other ways, alcohol had already begun to affect my life. My grades in school were getting progressively worse as my drinking increased. I no longer participated in sports or in any of the school clubs, and, although I worked 25 hours a week, I never had any money.

Reprinted from Brian, "Being a Child of an Alcoholic and Other Personal Stories," available at www.teenvoice.com/specials/drinking/articles/alcohol.html. Reprinted with permission from Teenvoice.

My focus had shifted from healthy adolescent hobbies to drinking. I drank and/or used some drug every day, was experiencing blackouts, and had begun to hurt some of the girls I was dating.

After graduating from high school, I went on to college. Once I located all of the local pubs, I rarely went to classes. In just a short time, I realized I would never do the work which was required of me here. I left school and began working in a clerical position at a major New York bank.

Alcohol Led to Troubling Situations

With the increased income, my drinking increased. At work, I soon found the people who partied like I did. It didn't take long before I was partying before work, during lunch, after work before the train home, and after dinner at the local bar. Some nights were fun, but the fun and games were not as frequent as they were in high school. In drunken stupors I would do things that hurt or embarrassed myself and my friends. Upon arising (sometimes the next afternoon) I was overwhelmed with feelings of shame and guilt that I felt could only be calmed with one thing, a drink. Alcohol was getting me into more and more situations I didn't want to be in. I was starting to think that maybe I was insane and drinking was the only thing holding me together.

Threats of being thrown out of my parents' house were constant. It seemed nothing mattered. I would be worried about being thrown out, losing my girlfriend, or losing my job—yet my focus was on getting drunk. My circle of friends was shrinking; sometimes I would be standing in a nice quiet bar getting drunk by myself when someone I knew would walk in. I didn't want to make conversation, all I wanted to do was drink but I would act as though I was glad to see them because I didn't want them to think I had a drinking problem.

Much of my time I spent trying to act so others could not see the effects of alcohol on me. Alcohol was depressing me. My fantasy had been to live on the beach in the Virgin Islands. (Ever since I started drinking I had never been out of my hometown.) It was now to live on the beach in the Islands and drink rum till I died. I thought this sounded tragically romantic. I hoped I would get a fatal disease so I could drink the way I wanted to and no one would bug me about it because I was dying anyway. Little did I know my alcoholism was a fatal disease and could kill me in time.

I finally sought help from what I thought was insanity. I figured I would end up in a straight-jacket in a padded cell. The psychiatrist I went to asked about alcohol and drugs. All I wanted to talk about was my other problems; he kept asking about alcohol and drugs.

Finally, he convinced me to try an AA meeting. My denial was furthered by my age and lack of a low-bottom story. I sat in meetings and compared, saying to myself, "I never drank Scotch in the morning," or

"I never got into a lot of trouble with the police. See, I'm not an alcoholic." AAs explained that some bottoms were lower than others, and that it was not how much I drank that mattered but how it affected me. I soon concentrated on identifying with the emotions and overall situation of the speakers instead of comparing details. If my bottom was low enough for me then it was low enough for AA. "The only requirement for membership is a desire to stop drinking," they told me. So I decided to give it a chance. Although I wasn't sure I was an alcoholic I was definitely "sick and tired of being sick and tired."

I started making meetings on a regular basis. I held onto the fact that I didn't have to be an alcoholic to attend AA meetings. I had the desire to stop drinking just for today. I used some of the phone numbers and accepted some of the caring that was given to me by other people in AA. It felt great to begin to understand that I wasn't bad or weak-willed; I was sick. Finally, on the Fourth of July, I was graced with independence from alcohol. I made 90 meetings in 90 days and got a sponsor. I made plenty of beginners' meetings; this was a new beginning. I followed all the suggestions that I could and became active in service.

My career has blossomed: from a clerk at a bank I am now an officer on the trading desk of a major brokerage firm. Although my relationships with my family, friends, and co-workers are not perfect or painless, they are no longer devastated by the effects of drinking and drugs.

Today I am first and foremost a member of AA, dedicated to recovery, service, and unity, but I am also now free to become whatever else I choose without the hindrance of alcohol.

WHY I DO NOT DRINK

Shannon Belmore

In the following selection, Shannon Belmore details why she has decided to resist the pro-drinking message that colleges often send. According to Belmore, because she comes from an alcoholic family, she knows the damage that alcohol can cause. Belmore contends that drinking in moderation is acceptable but that teenagers and young adults should not feel that the only way to fit in is by drinking. At the time this selection was written, Belmore was a journalism student at Ryerson Polytechnic University in Toronto, Ontario, Canada.

"What! You don't drink!?"

This is probably the most common phrase I hear now that I am in university.

At the end of each August, first year university students across Ontario pack their bags and leave home. For many, FROSH week is the beginning of the everlasting party that their newfound freedom will provide. For others, like myself, FROSH week means trying to fit in as a non-drinker. My worries began in early August when I received a letter written by the president of the Journalism Course Union (JCU). The letter described the functions of the JCU and how to become a member.

It concluded with these words of wisdom: ". . . [when] you're coming home late, and likely drunk too . . . we'll retire to the Library (a pub where beer is more prevalent than books) . . . to stack up the empty pitchers."

A Campus That Encourages Drinking

I knew then that fitting in would be harder than I had anticipated. FROSH week confirmed my fears. Of the ten nighttime activities that took place during the first seven days at Ryerson, only three were non-drinking events.

Many of the events during the week took place at Oakham House. Being a first year Ryerson student, I was unsure what went on there. I searched through all my flyers and pamphlets, which consisted mostly of advertisements for various clubs and bars, and finally found an article on Oakham House.

Reprinted from Shannon Belmore, "You Don't Drink?" available at www.drinksmart.org/belmore.html. Reprinted with permission from Young People's Press.

In an article in the "SoapBox," a newsletter produced by RyeSac (Ryerson Students' Administrative Council), it stated that Oakham House and its pub "give Ryerson students a place to call their own." At first I was thrilled with the idea that there was a place where students could go to relax and watch television. However, the article went on to describe the basement pub's decor which "resembles an old English watering hole," and to suggest that students should not miss Thursday pub nights or "you'll be kicking yourself all year." It's all too frustrating for non-drinkers. And I am much more upset with the assumption that every student drinks, than with the drinking itself.

Knowing the Dangers of Alcohol

I come from an alcoholic family. I know the damage that alcohol can cause, so to see so many young adults potentially ruining their lives scares me. I am not against drinking in moderation, nor do I see any problems in drinking socially. The problem arises, however, when students begin to feel that the only way to have fun or to fit in at social events is to drink.

It is not too hard to make friends in university, especially if you live in residence. But weekends pose a few problems for non-drinkers. When Friday rolls around, the offers to attend various clubs are endless. My response is usually "no, but thanks for asking."

This is not to say that if you don't drink you can't go out to a bar with your friends. However, for those of us who don't drink, paying a cover charge to spend an evening watching people get "loaded" is not appealing.

I'm glad I don't drink because, frankly, I could not afford to even if I wanted to. And I am not the only one counting my pennies to get through university. Drinking, particularly in clubs, is very expensive and creates a lot of economic problems for students who drink. With the high cost of university and college life, it is next to impossible for the average student to be able to afford to go out drinking on a weekly basis. Yet many, many students do.

Choosing Between Drinking and Learning

What this usually means for the drinker is that something else must be sacrificed. For some, it may simply mean spending less money on Christmas gifts, but, for others, it may mean not having enough money left for textbooks or even for the second tuition payment. A semester of drinking and partying can leave some students with no money and no education.

Of course, there are a number of students who are able to budget and spend wisely when it comes to drinking. They are able to drink in moderation and have a good time.

There are also students who don't drink and are able to have an enjoyable time at university, although they are more likely to have a hard time fitting in. To survive their post-secondary education, these students have to learn to accept the fact that drinking is prevalent at many functions, but that they have the right to choose whether or not they want to take part.

It would be nice if more people would recognize that not everyone at university drinks, and that more campus activities should be organized for non-drinkers. As for me, well, I won't be "kicking myself" at the end of the year for not going to "Thursday pub nights," but that doesn't mean I won't have had a good time.

My Son Was a Teenage Alcoholic

Marion W.

In the following selection, Marion W. recounts her decision to place her fifteen-year-old son in a rehabilitation center when his alcoholism made him suicidal. She notes that religion helped her realize that she could not help her son by herself. Marion also explains how the organization Al-Anon, which helps families and friends cope with the problem drinking of relatives and friends, provided support for her as she dealt with her son's alcoholism. The experience made her want to stay active in Al-Anon and help other families faced with similar situations, Marion writes.

Last night I sat behind a couple who attended our meeting regularly for almost a year. It has been wonderful to watch them grow. The topic for discussion was, "How have you used Al-Anon in your life this week?"

As we went around the room, the man shared that his 15-year-old stepson relapsed this week. They had to have him arrested and placed in a special Twelve Step program. He mentioned how easy it was to make their decision because of what they heard in Al-Anon. The woman added, "Thank goodness for Al-Anon," and discussion continued around the room.

A Son's Problems with Alcohol

My mind flashed back to the day I placed my own son in a rehabilitation program when he was 15. I could feel the heavy, painful ache as I recalled the door with metal bars clanging shut and locking behind me. I felt the same knot in my stomach and the lump in my throat. I remember the empty months and years that followed, too. In my desolation I feared that I wasn't doing the right thing. I wondered if I had just loved him a little better, would he be okay.

My son's disease was not accepted by the family. We weren't supposed to talk about it. My husband said if I would just stop overreacting and be a better mother, everything would be all right. He didn't believe my son needed rehabilitation, but my son begged for help because he tried to kill himself and could not stop drinking. I didn't have Al-Anon then.

Reprinted from Marion W., "I Know," *The Forum*, January 2000. Reprinted with permission from *The Forum*, Al-Anon Family Group Headquarters, Inc., Virginia Beach, VA.

When I looked at the woman in my meeting and saw her lip quivering from trying to keep her composure, I knew this is what it's all about. After I had been in Al-Anon for a while, I made a decision. Alcoholism affected both my family and my spouse's family for many generations, and with my son's disease we all experienced severe pain and confusion. I knew all this suffering needed to lead toward something positive, and I was going to make that happen.

I made a commitment to always be an active Al-Anon member. I would involve myself in service in order to keep Al-Anon alive for those who needed it in the future. I promised to attend at least one meeting every week and to pass on to others what I felt so blessed to receive.

When the meeting closed, I walked up to this woman and said, "What a loving, caring mother you are. Your son is so lucky to have you." She looked at me and said, "It was so hard."

Turning to God for Help

As we hugged and I held her in my arms, no words were necessary except when I said, "I know." After many months of sharing at meetings, we knew what was in each other's heart. We both felt the enormous pain that comes when a mother sees her child on the destructive path where this disease leads. We both knew how deep within ourselves we had to reach to be able to say, "I love my son enough to let him go." We realized a bandage and a kiss wouldn't heal our child this time. He needed the wisdom and assistance of those who could really help. This was the heartrending point when I realized I can't, but God can, and I need to Let Go and Let God or my child will surely die from this disease.

I shared something with her that someone once said to me. "By not enabling, by letting go and letting your son face the consequences of his actions, you give him the opportunity to grow up and become a responsible, loving, caring adult." I was also able to share with her how my son, who is now in his 30s, and his alcoholic wife no longer drink. They have a wonderful, loving family and a close relationship with their Higher Power. Their three children are growing up in a loving, caring atmosphere.

The last 16 years haven't always been easy, but my son and I have always been able to say, "I love you," with deep meaning. Through it all, he has always said, "Thank goodness you are in Al-Anon. If I ever need to talk, I know you will understand." Each of us had a Higher Power to lean on when the going got rough. We could rely on that Higher Power when we didn't know which way to turn.

God helped me separate the disease from the child and has allowed both of us to know and share our love for each other no matter what else is going on. My gift is to remember where I used to be and to know how I got where I am today, so I can and will pass it on.

Drunk Driving Brings a Lifetime of Pain

Casey McCary Bloom

Alcohol abuse can have serious consequences. In the following narrative, Casey McCary Bloom discusses his decision to drive drunk as a college student, an incident that led to the death of a teenaged girl and Bloom's being sentenced to twenty-one years in prison. He concludes that while the physical punishment is severe, it does not compare to the grief he feels over his mistake. Bloom is a prisoner at Jackson County Jail in Marianna, Florida.

In one blink of an eye my college career violently was taken away from me. Fear, sadness and a painful sense of confusion is cast over me as I lie here in a cold, lonely place called prison.

I am facing 21 years in prison for one mistake I made and regret— to drink and drive. I am going to tell you a true story that ends with me being where I am now.

I don't want you to take this lightly. I, like many of you, was a college student with my whole life ahead of me. The choice I made to get behind the wheel of a car drunk took every bit of my life, along with a piece of my heart, away from me.

A Weekend Celebration

One weekend, seven of us decided to take a trip down from college to my parents' beach cottage in Panama City [Florida]. It was the last weekend of the summer, and there were no intentions of getting out of control.

We all just wanted to have a nice relaxing weekend away from all the wild parties that go on during football season and before kicking off the school year. We were three guys and four girls celebrating our last weekend before beginning our sophomore year.

Because of afternoon classes, we did not arrive in Panama City until late Friday night. We unloaded the cars and prepared for bed. I did not know then, but it was the last decent night's sleep I would have.

We got up the next morning, loaded the cooler with beer and headed for the beach. We laughed, drank and exchanged stories from our freshman year. As the day drifted slowly to an end, we packed up

Reprinted from Casey McCary Bloom, "Drunk Driving Brings a Lifetime of Pain," February 19, 1997, available at www.alligator.org/edit/issues/97-sprg/970219/c02bloom. htm. Reprinted with permission from Campus Communications, Inc.

and headed for the house. We had no plans to go out on the town, just to cook out and relax as we sipped on ice cold beers. The night I would never forget had just begun.

After finishing an enormous meal, we continued to drink and dance until 1:00 A.M. We had to get back to school early the next day, so we decided to fill the car with gas and get more cigarettes that night.

A Fatal Car Accident

My friend and I hopped in his truck, me in the driver's seat and he in the passenger seat, and headed to an all-night convenience store.

We found one store open about two miles down the road. We pulled in, gassed up and headed back to the beach house. It was a straight shot, just a few minutes down a four-lane highway.

As we approached the turn leading back to the beach house, my life flashed before my eyes in one terrifying fraction of a second. Our truck violently crashed into another car carrying four teenagers.

Young, pretty, 17-year-old Donn'elle McGraw, who was in the back seat of the other car, was killed instantly. The other back seat passenger, Mark Weber, was critically injured and was in a coma for a week.

The passenger in my car went through the windshield. This horrifying experience seemed to be a nightmare. It wasn't until I was told Donn'elle had died that I became aware that this nightmare was indeed a horrible reality.

I will never forget the screaming and crying that I heard that night. When the police arrived, I was questioned, handcuffed and arrested. I was charged with two felony counts—driving-under-the-influence (DUI) manslaughter and DUI serious bodily injury.

I was booked into Bay County jail. When I woke the next day, I felt indescribable sadness, depression and anxiety. Not only had I taken the life of a young girl, but my life had been taken as well.

Following the accident, after spending two nights in jail, I was released on bail for an entire year. I may have been out of jail, but there was not one day that passed that I didn't grieve over the death of the girl and the sorrow of her family and friends.

Physical and Emotional Punishments

I have had dreadful nightmares since the accident, leaving me frightened and in tears. I have carried this burden with me for a year and will continue to carry it for as long as I live.

Exactly one year from the accident, I was tried and convicted of both felony charges, which carry a sentence of 14-and-a-half to 24 years in prison. I will serve 21 years, or 85 percent of this sentence.

But no physical punishment I receive will compare to the emotional punishment I have been going through and will go through for the rest of my life. There is not one person or family that should ever have to go through what the families of the victims and I have been through. It just isn't worth it.

I ask that you please hear what I have written and understand the irreversible consequences of drinking and driving. I was a college student who thought this could never happen to me. Well, as you know, I was dead wrong. I had no intentions of ever hurting anyone. But because of the decision I made to get behind the wheel of a car, my life has been permanently affected.

Don't make the mistake I did. One simple phone call or cab fare may seem a little inconvenient, but will save you from a lifetime of pain.

I Lost Two Friends in Drunk Driving Accidents

Jenee Rager

Jenee Rager explains how she had a serious drinking problem as a teenager but stopped drinking after losing two friends in separate drunk driving accidents. Following the second accident, in which her friend decided to drive home by himself rather than call for a ride, Rager decided to begin a program to eliminate drunk driving in her town. Rager is an employee with the Kansas Council on Developmental Disabilities and a counselor for Teenadviceonline.org, which provides advice and support for problems experienced by teenagers.

There was a time when alcohol was my closest friend. I loved nothing more than its sticky warmth coating my throat and stomach, and the light-headed feeling it gave me. I needed it to be outgoing. I thought people liked me better when I drank. I told myself every lie known to man rather than face the fact I was an alcoholic.

The Experiences of a Teenage Alcoholic

I had my first drink shortly after I turned thirteen. I thought the Wild Berry wine cooler somehow eased my problems. Even if the peace of mind was only momentary, I thought it was worth it at the time.

At first I only drank occasionally, in social situations. Then it became every weekend. By the time I was sixteen I was a full-fledged alcoholic. I rarely went a day without at least one swallow of liquor. I'd long since moved on from wine coolers to hard liquor. I downed screwdrivers, and Ron Rico's and Coke like water. The stronger they were the better, it meant I'd forget all my other problems even quicker. Unfortunately it also meant my common sense would also disappear rather rapidly.

There were many mornings that I woke up and couldn't remember long periods from the night before. I counted on my friends to tease me about my behavior the next day to fill in the blanks. I laughed along with them like I'd remembered all along. "Yeah, I know I flashed the football team. Of course I remember puking on the

Reprinted from Jenee Rager, "The World Doesn't Need to Lose Any More Justins and Hillarys," available at www.teenadviceonline.org/articles/drinkingdrive.html. Reprinted with permission from Teen Advice Online.

McDonald's counter. You're right, it was funny when I did that line dance on the hood of my car." I lied to them because it was easier than admitting to myself how bad my drinking had become.

Of course I had periods where I didn't drink for awhile. I was sober for two weeks after I ended up in the emergency room puking up blood. I even went six whole months without a drink when a boyfriend said I had to choose him or the booze. Once he was gone I hit the bottle even harder though. I had to make up for lost time.

Miraculously I stuck strictly with alcohol. I never tried drugs, and smoked only on rare occasions when I was trying to impress someone. Despite my binges I managed to keep my grades up and remain popular at school. Besides my health the only thing that drinking forced me to sacrifice was basketball. When I started my freshman year there was talk of me playing for college. By my junior year I didn't even bother to go out. In some ways this was good, in others it was bad. I thought alcoholics lost everything that mattered to them and I hadn't reached that point yet.

How Two Friends Died

In November of 1996 I made the decision not to drink and drive. One of my sister's friends was coming home from a party. She was seated on the console of her boyfriend's car and they swerved out of their lane and hit a sand truck head on. Hillary was thrown head first from the car, hit the sand truck with her back, and was finally killed when she was impaled by a fence post and her head was slammed into the ground so hard it buried it four inches underground. Her death was horrible enough to make me give up driving when I was drunk but it wasn't enough to make me quit drinking. I really didn't know her that well, plus there were too many other factors that played a part in the accident. Hillary wasn't wearing a seat belt, it was icy outside, and it was a foggy night. I couldn't bring myself to admit she was a victim of a drunk driving accident instead of merely an unfortunate traffic accident.

Then in September 1997 tragedy struck again. This time it was enough to wake me up and admit I had a problem. On Friday my friend Justin found out that he made the Kansas University (KU) basketball team as a walk-on. Of course we needed to celebrate. His cousin (and my best friend), Eddie, knew about a party a few blocks from his house. So Justin picked us up in his truck and we went and celebrated. Close to 2:30 that morning Justin wanted to go. Eddie and I suggested that he just walk back to Ed's house with us and sleep there, but Justin said he had to go home. Since he wasn't supposed to drink during training, and we didn't want him to get a driving-under-the-influence conviction (DUI) and get caught, we suggested that he call someone to pick him up. He said it was too late and he didn't want to wake anyone up, besides he hadn't drank that much. So I gave him a hug, told him I was really happy he made the team, buck-led his seatbelt for him and watched him drive away. I had no idea that it would be the last time I'd see him.

The next morning Eddie's mom woke us up really early. She called us to the kitchen table where his brothers were waiting and broke the news to us all at once. Justin had been killed on the way home. The police think he was leaning over to adjust his stereo and didn't notice the curve ahead. Even though he hadn't had that much to drink it was enough to slow his reflexes, (reflexes that were fast enough that he had made our state's best basketball team) so he wasn't able to turn the wheel in time. His truck struck the center wall at such speed that he was thrown right out of his seat belt, across two lanes of highway into the ravine on the other side. Witnesses thought it was a deer that had been struck. Even though they were sure he had just gotten scared and left the scene of the accident, the police decided to look for him in the ravine when they didn't find him in his truck. They found his body about twenty feet down the embankment, they confirmed it was him through the driver's license in his pocket because his face was unrecog-nizable. Unlike Hillary he had at least been killed instantly.

This time I couldn't blame any outside factors. Justin had his seat belt on, the roads were dry, the sky was clear. The only thing to blame for his death was the one thing I loved so much, alcohol.

The World Doesn't Need to Lose Any More Justins and Hillarys

Eddie and I haven't had a drink since that night. I'm sorry it took the deaths of two wonderful teenagers to wake me up but it did. After Justin died I started a program to help eliminate drunk driving in my town. Groups of two go into local bars and dance clubs and offer to give free rides home to anyone who needs them. We also leave a list of our numbers with the bar owner and doormen. They can call us if no one from the team shows up or there aren't enough people to drive everyone that needs a ride home. The project has gotten a lot of word of mouth from local youth and we get calls from people at par-ties and stuff too. It doesn't matter what time it is, if someone calls us we go. I've had to get out of my bed at 4:00 on a work night to pick people up from the after hours parties. I'm tired the next day but it's worth it. It's my way of making things up to Justin.

I'm not going to lie; there have been a few times since I've quit drinking that I've been sitting in a bar waiting to take people home and the urge to drink will hit me. All I have to do is think about Justin and Hillary though and it quickly disappears. I know I have an addic-tive personality; if I drink I won't be able to control it, so I just don't drink. It also helps me that so many people look up to me for what I'm doing with the driving program; if I have even one shot I'm going to let a lot of people down.

I know there are hundreds of people out there who are like I used to be. They won't admit how bad their problem is. I hope it doesn't take a tragedy for them to realize it like it did me. I also realize that there are a lot of people out there like Justin, who think they're doing their families a favor by not waking them up to come and get them after they've been drinking. But what kind of favor did he really do them? Don't you think that his parents would rather have been woken up every night for the rest of their lives to come and get him rather than have to bury him before his nineteenth birthday? It hurts them so bad to think he was so afraid of letting them down that he wouldn't even call to ask for help when he needed it.

So next time you're about to have a drink, or the next time you think you are okay to drive home after a night of partying think it over. The world doesn't need to lose any more Justins and Hillarys.

Chapter 4

Solving the Problem of Teen Alcoholism

ALCOHOLIC BEVERAGE ADVERTISING SHOULD BE RESTRICTED

Laurie Leiber

In the following article, Laurie Leiber contends that alcohol abuse among teenagers can be reduced if the government places restrictions on the advertising of alcoholic beverages. According to Leiber, research has shown that television beer commercials lead to favorable attitudes toward drinking among children. She maintains that the liquor industry's voluntary advertising codes have not prevented those companies from creating commercials that use cartoon animals to sell their beverages or from airing the advertisements when young people are most likely to be watching. Leiber suggests that the Federal Communications Commission should institute policies that will limit the exposure of adolescents to such advertising. Leiber was the director of the now-defunct Center on Alcohol Advertising, a project of San Francisco General Hospital's Trauma Foundation.

For nearly two decades, two U.S. Surgeon Generals—C. Everett Koop and Antonia Novello—and numerous public health organizations—including the American Academy of Pediatrics, the National Parent Teachers Association, the American Medical Association, and Mothers Against Drunk Driving—have called upon manufacturers of alcoholic beverages to advertise more responsibly. National polls show that Americans increasingly favor either restricting or banning broadcast alcohol advertising.

But despite this widespread support for advertising reform, the alcohol industry—using its considerable political clout and such pre-emptive PR strategies as public-service campaigns and voluntary advertising codes—has averted government limits. During the same 20 years, public health advocates working at local, state, and national levels began implementing a new approach to preventing alcohol-related problems. This new public health response is based on a substantial and growing body of evidence that limiting both alcohol

Reprinted from Laurie Leiber, "Should the Government Restrict Advertising of Alcoholic Beverages? Yes," *Priorities for Health*, 1997. Reprinted with permission from *Priorities*, a publication of the American Council on Science and Health (ACSH), 1995 Broadway, 2nd Floor, New York, NY 10023-5800. Learn more about ACSH online at www.acsh.org and www.prioritiesforhealth.com.

advertising and alcohol availability and raising alcohol taxes decreases alcohol-related problems.

Alcohol Advertising Influences Children

Alcohol-industry representatives often cite the incompleteness of the research record on alcohol advertising as proof that alcohol promotion has no impact on consumption. However, to clarify the impact of promotional efforts—efforts on which the industry spends $2 billion annually—independent researchers have begun to frame questions and pursue studies on the relationship between alcohol advertising and behavior and health. Although more research is needed, there is strong scientific evidence that the effects of alcohol advertising, like the effects of tobacco advertising, are not limited to brand selection by adults. Research conducted by Joel W. Grube and Lawrence Wallack suggests that awareness of TV beer commercials leads to favorable beliefs about drinking in children 10 to 12 years old and increases their intention to drink as adults. Henry Saffer compared motor-vehicle deaths with quarterly measures for broadcast advertising in 75 media markets over a three-year period. He concluded that a ban on broadcast alcohol advertising would save 2,000 to 3,000 people annually from death due to alcohol-related motor-vehicle crashes.

In the past, alcoholic-beverage producers have argued that their voluntary public-service campaigns are more effective at decreasing alcohol-related problems than are government-imposed limits on alcohol advertising. But while public-service messages may engender goodwill for the companies sponsoring them, researchers [William] DeJong, [Charles K.] Atkin, and [Lawrence] Wallack have described these "responsible drinking" spots as thinly disguised drinking promotions. The longest-running campaign, Anheuser-Busch's "Know When to Say When," omits that sometimes it is not safe to imbibe at all. The campaign also leaves "when" undefined. At a recent Anheuser-Busch board meeting, officers opposed a shareholder request to add the U.S. Dietary Guidelines definition of moderation to the company's alcohol awareness materials.

Manufacturers of alcoholic beverages also assert that, because responsible advertising is advantageous to the industry, government-imposed restrictions are unnecessary. Trade groups representing the three branches of the alcohol industry (wine, beer, and distilled spirits) have adopted voluntary advertising codes. But these voluntary standards have not prevented the brewers from turning Halloween into a beer festival, marketing malt liquor on MTV, or using cute cartoon animals in commercials aired on TV during peak viewing times for young people.

Neither did the industry's standards prevent liquor producers from ending their decades-long voluntary ban on broadcast liquor commercials. After Seagram broke the ban in June 1996, the Distilled Spirits Council of the United States (DISCUS) simply rewrote its Code of Good Practice. Since then, commercials for Seagram's Crown Royal whiskey that feature dogs, ducks, and peacocks have appeared during weekend telecasts of college and professional sports events, broadcasts of ABC's Monday Night Football, and a 7:00 P.M. *Cosby Show* rerun. Print ads for liquor—a magazine mainstay—appear in periodicals such as *Spin*, nearly half of whose readers are under 21, and *Allure*, 44 percent of whose readers are underage. Billboard and print ads for Gordon's gin feature a cartoon boar. Quirky cutout characters populate Tanqueray vodka ads.

Ineffective Guidelines

In terms of both content and placement, manufacturers of alcoholic beverages find few real limitations in the industry's voluntary advertising guidelines. Research conducted in spring 1996 by the Center on Alcohol Advertising showed that children aged 9 to 11 are more familiar with the Budweiser frogs than they are with Smokey the Bear or Tony the Tiger.

Anheuser-Busch, the maker of Budweiser, responded to widespread criticism of the frog commercials by citing the adult appeal of the croaking amphibians. According to the Beer Institute ad code, if a symbol or character appeals to persons over 21, beer makers are free to use that image in their promotions no matter how much the image appeals to children.

The industry's voluntary standards also address settings in which alcohol ads should not appear. According to the Beer Institute's code, beer advertising is inappropriate for TV programs most of whose audience is "reasonably expected to be below the legal purchase age." However, both *Advertising Age* and *The Wall Street Journal* have reported that beer ads on MTV reached viewers 69 percent of whom were below the legal drinking age of 21.

The pertinent section of the Beer Institute's Advertising and Marketing Code reads: "Beer advertising and marketing materials should not be placed in magazines, newspapers, television programs, radio programs, or other media where most of the audience is reasonably expected to be below the legal purchase age." This means that the Institute does not consider an ad placement questionable unless at least half the audience is underage. In December 1996, possibly because it foresaw the *AdAge* and *WSJ* reports, Anheuser-Busch moved its ads from MTV to VH-1, a cable station whose proportion of adult viewers is higher. Five months later, Miller, the number-two brewing company, announced that it would follow suit.

While broadcasters and advertisers routinely use detailed reports of audience demographics to develop marketing strategies, this information is not generally available to people concerned about the impact of broadcast advertising on the welfare of children or of the public. The "sentinel effect" of the *AdAge* and *WSJ* reports is temporary and narrow, affecting only a handful of cable stations.

Steps the Government Should Take

Our government should mandate monitoring the reach of alcohol commercials and should hold broadcasters responsible for limiting young people's exposure to such advertising. By law, television and radio stations licensed to broadcast on the public airwaves must do so in the public interest. The Federal Communications Commission (FCC) does not collect information on the frequency of alcohol commercials; nor does it gather age information on the viewers of such ads. The FCC could use such information to set goals for decreasing youth exposure. The agency could also require broadcasters to provide equal time for health-and-safety messages when alcohol commercials air during primetime or sports programs that reach large numbers of underage viewers.

While broadcast ads probably constitute their most powerful marketing tool, producers of alcoholic beverages use various other media to reach young consumers. Control of unethical alcohol advertising in these other media will require different strategies: An ordinance in Baltimore restricts billboard ads for alcoholic beverages to certain areas of the city. Citizens of Marin County, California, petitioned to eliminate prizes "decorated" with beer logos from the midway at their county fair. In 1996 groups in several states asked their alcoholic-beverage control agencies to ban Halloween-theme displays for beer in convenience stores and groceries. And the Federal Trade Commission's vote to restrict the use of R.J. Reynolds' Joe Camel character may open the door to similar action against "unfair" alcohol ads.

Advocates of public health and safety should press for mandatory limits on alcohol promotions that reach underage consumers, as manufacturers of alcoholic beverages have demonstrated that they cannot be trusted to market their products responsibly. The manufacturers are well aware that maintaining industry profits depends on "recruiting" young drinkers. Most Americans "mature out" of heavy drinking by their mid to late 20s, but an analysis of American alcohol consumption shows that heavy drinkers dominate the market: A mere 5 percent of the population drinks 53 percent of all the alcohol consumed in this country. Because nearly half of all young people in the U.S. begin drinking before they have graduated from junior high school, competition for market share among the next group of heavy drinkers means attracting people well below the legal drinking age. And people who begin drinking when they are very young are the likeliest lifelong heavy drinkers.

No one should expect alcoholic-beverage manufacturers to end their aggressive targeting of young people voluntarily. The industry is fiercely competitive and thus far has not placed children's welfare above profits. The costs to the United States of alcohol consumption are tremendous, with recent estimates approaching $100 billion per year. Our government has a legitimate interest in reducing both these costs and the human costs of alcohol-related illness, injury, and death. Restricting the promotion of alcoholic beverages, and particularly their promotion to children, should be part of a comprehensive strategy to abate alcohol-related problems through policy reform.

Liquor Advertising Should Not Be Restricted

Doug Bandow

In the following selection, Doug Bandow, a senior fellow at the Cato Institute, rejects the argument that advertising by liquor companies should be restricted due to its adverse impact on young people. Bandow insists there is no evidence that such advertising increases alcohol consumption among teenagers. Moreover, he asserts that the First Amendment gives liquor companies the right to advertise their products and the government should not infringe upon that right. Rather than ban advertisement that might target adolescents, Bandow concludes, the government should punish the sale of alcohol to minors. The Cato Institute supports public policies that limit the role of government and protect individual liberties.

You'd think cocaine traffickers had taken over Madison Avenue. Shortly after we toast the new year, the Federal Communications Commission (FCC) plans to launch an investigation. The Federal Trade Commission (FTC) has already done so. The president and Senate majority leader have issued threats; newspaper columnists and editorial writers have fulminated. What's the problem? Joseph E. Seagram & Sons has begun advertising its Crown Royal Canadian whiskey on TV, breaking the industry's voluntary ban on broadcast ads.

Advertising and the First Amendment

Curious are the ubiquitous wailing and gnashing of teeth that have greeted Seagram's decision. One of the hallmarks of a free society is the right to sell products to willing consumers. A second feature, guaranteed by the First Amendment, is the right to advertise products that are legal. Hence, beer and wine are not only available to adults, but also seen in print and on television. In fact, the beer industry alone spends more than $600 million annually on advertising.

Why not liquor, then? The FTC, it seems, is concerned that children may see Seagram's ads. For the same reason the agency is also investigating the Stroh Brewery Co.'s advertising of malt liquor, which has a

Excerpted from Doug Bandow, "Liquor Ads on the Rocks," *The Wall Street Journal*, January 22, 1997. Reprinted from *The Wall Street Journal* © 1997 Dow Jones & Company, Inc. All rights reserved.

higher alcohol content than most beers. FCC Chairman Reed Hundt says he too wants to restrict liquor ads, even though the FCC has not traditionally regulated advertising. The baying legislative hounds are using the same paternalistic excuse—liquor advertising for anyone at any time might be seen by children. Rep. Joseph Kennedy [Democrat, Massachusetts] contends that the industry's voluntary ban "shielded generations of America's children from the kind of predatory broadcast advertising practices that American brewers use to mass-market beer." For this reason, Rep. Kennedy has introduced the "Just Say No" Act to outlaw liquor (but not beer) ads, to "send a clear message that liquor profiteering at the expense of America's children is . . . unacceptable.". . .

Impact on Youth Is Unclear

Of course, few people really favor "liquor profiteering at the expense of America's children." And that isn't what Seagram is doing by advertising a legal product used by tens of millions of adults.

First, it isn't clear that advertising has a substantial impact on the demand for alcohol by either adults or children. Companies like Seagram use ads more to increase market share than to turn teetotalers into drinkers. A decade ago, a more sober FTC admitted that there was "no reliable basis to conclude that alcohol advertising significantly affects consumption, let alone abuse" and that "absent such evidence, there is no basis for concluding that rules banning or otherwise limiting alcohol advertising would offer significant protection to the public."

Second, even if advertising did substantially affect demand, what would be wrong with distillers encouraging people to use more of their products? Some people drink too much, but that's not the fault of advertising. Alcoholics don't need to be urged to take a drink. Most Americans enjoy drinking, and drink responsibly. They have a right to receive information about different drinks from the sellers, unimpeded by government.

If Washington can ban the advertising of products at will, what is to stop the government from deciding to forbid auto makers from marketing fast cars, or low-mileage ones, or outlaw butter ads, or bar the broadcast of any ad that encourages selfishness and consumerism? Every private economic decision would become an arbitrary political one.

Third, the fact that children might see alcohol ads doesn't justify treating everyone like children by banning such advertising. Parents have the primary responsibility for protecting their kids and guiding them into adulthood.

No Reason to Ban Ads

Government's principal duty is to protect people in the exercise of their freedom, including enjoying a drink or two, in daily life. To circumscribe those rights in the name of protecting children would violate the very purpose of government.

Few products exist that could not, if misused, hurt children. Cars, riding mowers, high-fat food, computers: almost every good advertised on the airwaves may have some inadvertent adverse effect on the young. That's no excuse for banning ads. Government needs to punish abusive, not innocent, behavior—say, selling alcohol of any sort to minors—rather than advertising whiskey. The case for limited paternalism focused on children does not justify pervasive paternalism penalizing adults as well.

However unpopular Seagram's decision to advertise its products on television, in a free society this sort of choice belongs to the company. If the political mob now forming in Washington compels Seagram to back down, the American Constitution, not the Canadian company, will be the primary loser.

HOW COLLEGES HAVE RESPONDED TO TEENAGE DRINKING

Karen Lee Scrivo

In the following selection, Karen Lee Scrivo details the ways in which different colleges have tried to reduce the problem of underage drinking. Some colleges have banned alcohol at campus events, while other universities have implemented tougher penalties against underage drinkers. In addition, because fraternities and sororities are often linked to heavy drinking, some of those organizations have responded by banning alcohol from their parties and houses. Scrivo is a writer for *CQ Researcher*.

Leslie Anne Baltz had been drinking heavily before she died November [1997] in a fall down a flight of stairs. In fact, the 21-year-old honors student may have died after observing what some students claim is a longtime custom among University of Virginia (UVA) seniors—the "fourth-year fifth"—downing a fifth of liquor before the football team's last home game.

Baltz's friends left her sleeping on an upstairs couch and went to the game. Upon returning, they found Baltz unconscious at the foot of the stairs. She was rushed to the university medical center, where she died. Her blood-alcohol level was 0.27 percent—more than three times the state's legal limit for intoxication.

Tragedies in Virginia

Two days later, Susan J. Grossman discussed Baltz's death with her "Substance Abuse and Society" class. Some students said it changed their outlook about drinking, but few actually planned to change their own drinking habits, recalls Grossman, associate director of the university's Institute for Substance Abuse Studies.

"They felt drinking was their choice," she says. "Some said, 'These things happen once in a while.' I was astounded. There is this feeling that they're invulnerable, that it can't happen to them."

Less than a month after Baltz's death, UVA students at a popular Charlottesville bar echoed those feelings of invincibility. Some said they drank heavily once or twice a week to relieve the stress of school and their personal lives. Steve Bremer, a third-year fraternity member,

Excerpted from Karen Lee Scrivo, "Drinking on Campus," *CQ Researcher*, March 20, 1998. Reprinted with permission.

said he got intoxicated six or seven times a month. "It's absolutely the norm at UVA," he said.

Like Grossman's students, few of the students at the bar planned to change their drinking habits, but many said they would take better care of their drunken friends. "I'll never leave a friend alone in that condition again," said Dave Clark, another junior.

Baltz, of Reston, Virginia, was the fifth Virginia college student in less than two months to die following a night of heavy drinking. A few weeks earlier, Melinda Somers, a Virginia Polytechnic Institute (VPI) freshman, apparently rolled out of bed and through an open eighth-floor dormitory window. She had been drinking heavily at a Halloween party. She died the day before her 19th birthday.

Somers' death prompted Virginia's attorney general to form a task force of college presidents, students and health experts to find ways of curbing alcohol abuse on campuses. UVA President John T. Casteen III sent out a letter after Baltz's death, calling for the community "to learn how to change a culture that too often considers alcohol abuse a normal stage of growing up."

The deaths of Somers and Baltz were the latest in a string of campus alcohol-related tragedies. In September [1997], an 18-year-old Massachusetts Institute of Technology (MIT) freshman honors student—Scott Krueger—died after an off-campus party at the Boston house of the Phi Gamma Delta fraternity, which he was pledging. He had an alcohol level of 0.41—more than five times the legal limit. A month earlier, Benjamin Wynne died after a party at the Sigma Alpha Epsilon fraternity house at Louisiana State University (LSU). Wynne, a fraternity pledge, had an alcohol level of 0.58, nearly six times the state's legal limit. . . .

How Colleges Approach the Problem

The recent spate of alcohol-related student deaths has renewed calls for banning alcohol on college campuses. While most undergraduates cannot legally buy alcohol, many still drink. The clash between legality and reality sparks debate on whether banning alcohol reduces irresponsible drinking or just encourages out-of-control, off-campus parties like the one that ended tragically August [1997] for LSU student Wynne. The 20-year-old drank himself to death with a potent mixture of 151-proof rum, whiskey and liqueur at a seven-hour off-campus fraternity party. LSU had banned alcohol at fraternities and campus events in an effort to curb campus drinking.

In view of such tragedies, some college administrators think that allowing on-campus drinking for students 21 and older would at least let the school regulate it. Salisbury State University in Maryland, for example, converted a dining hall into a bar in an effort to control how much students drink and keep them from driving after drinking. Unlike regular bars, the Crossroads Pub doesn't have a "happy hour" or reduced-price specials that encourage drinking. At Johns Hopkins University in Baltimore, a former security officer manages the school's bar. But underage drinking problems closed the Underground, a bar at Brown University.

"I favor campus pubs, if they are strictly enforced," [William] Dejong [director of the Higher Education Center for Alcohol and Other Drug Prevention] says. "Even students under 21 enjoy them. There is food and entertainment. Nothing is accomplished by pushing alcohol entirely off campus."

But Harvard's [Henry] Wechsler urges universities to stop the flow of alcohol on campus. He also urges colleges to crack down on fraternities and sororities that encourage binge and underage drinking, to work with local police to keep local bars from serving underage drinkers and to avoid sending "mixed messages" about drinking.

"If you let them drink on campus, it doesn't mean they'll only drink on campus," he said.

MIT announced tougher penalties for underage drinking in February [1998] following the death [in fall 1997] of 18-year-old Scott Krueger, who lost consciousness after heavy drinking at an off-campus party held by a fraternity he was pledging. He never woke up. [During the 1997–98] school year, another MIT student was hospitalized for alcohol poisoning and 22 others were charged with alcohol violations. Under the school's new policy, violators face disciplinary action ranging from mandatory counseling and loss of housing to $1,500 in fines and expulsion.

"There is no question that the events of last fall highlighted this gap in our overall alcohol policy," said Rosalind Williams, MIT's dean of students and undergraduate education. The new system will "demonstrate to local governments, to the nation at large and to ourselves that we can govern ourselves responsibly."

In December [1997], not long after the alcohol-related deaths at UVA and VPI, police cracked down on underage drinking at a fraternity party at Virginia Commonwealth University in Richmond and arrested 53 people for rowdiness and underage drinking, giving new urgency to the task force on campus alcohol abuse.

While the Promising Practices study rated UVA's alcohol-abuse program as one of the 12 most comprehensive in the country, the percentage of heavy drinkers at the university jumped from 47 percent in 1996 to 51 percent in 1997, according to the school's Institute of Substance Abuse Studies.

"There is a strong drinking environment here," Grossman says. "Our goal is to change the environment."

The university has not tried to stop drinking but rather to reduce abuse and make sure people are safe, she says. The university program includes training for resident advisers, student athlete mentors, peer prevention, a hospitality committee that holds alcohol-free events,

Drug Awareness Week, education and information for fraternities and sororities and classes on substance abuse.

Tougher Policies

Vanderbilt University in Nashville, Tennessee, tightened its alcohol policies after three students, all non-fraternity members, died [in 1997] in alcohol-related incidents. Students who use fake identification cards or devices for fast alcohol consumption, such as funnels, now face sanctions, and no alcohol is permitted in first-year dormitories.

But first-year students who want to drink just get fake IDs and drive to downtown bars a few blocks away, said David Burch, editor of the *Hustler*, the campus newspaper.

A *U.S. News & World Report* survey of more than 1,000 college presidents found that schools that allow drinking on campus are three times more likely to have high percentages of binge drinkers. The magazine also found that when schools included their alcohol policies and penalties in recruiting material, they were half as likely to have large numbers of binge drinkers.

The University of Rhode island, once considered a party school, bans drinking anywhere on campus for students under 21. Legal-age students are limited to one six-pack at a time in dorm rooms. Students with three violations of the restrictions are suspended. The policy has led to a reduction in alcohol-related violations such as vandalism and violence.

But even if such bans work, some question whether they send the right message. "Zero tolerance sounds great on paper, but it reinforces the mystique of intoxification," said a *Wall Street Journal* editorial after the death of Wynne of LSU.

Teach Responsible Drinking

Rather than banning alcohol, universities need to change student misperceptions that everyone drinks a lot, [Michael P.] Haines says, because they lead to a self-fulfilling prophesy.

Universities need to get the message out that most students—if they drink—drink responsibly, says Haines, a consultant to more than 30 schools, including California Polytech University, Montana State University and the University of Arizona.

At Northern Illinois, Haines' anti–alcohol abuse campaign included eye-catching ads and prizes for students who guessed the percentage of heavy drinkers on campus. In the process, students learned that most of their classmates, in fact, were not heavy drinkers, and student drinking decreased by a third, Haines says.

"Students will be more responsible about their drinking if they understand the situation," he says.

When it comes to heavy drinking, student fraternity leaders are at the head of the class. Nearly 74 percent said they had engaged in binge drinking, according to a 1994–1995 survey of more than 25,000 students at 61 colleges. Moreover, they reported having an average of 14 drinks each week, while non-fraternity members averaged six drinks.

"In other words, the leaders are participating in setting the norms of heavy drinking and behavioral loss of control," the study notes.

The study found that college women drank less than men, but that sorority leaders and active sorority members drank more than unaffiliated women. Nearly 55 percent of sorority leaders had engaged in binge drinking compared with 26 percent of those not in sororities.

"[T]he data indicated that students see alcohol as a vehicle of friendship, social activity and sexual opportunity, and these beliefs occur to a greater extent among Greeks than non-Greeks," the study said.

The 1993 Harvard study found similar fraternity and sorority drinking patterns. In fact, the rate was even higher for residents of fraternity and sorority houses—86 percent and 80 percent, respectively.

"The alcohol-use pattern [by Greeks] is higher," says George Mason's [professor David] Anderson, "but that's not to say they cause it. That's where the heavy drinkers are, and the other heavy drinkers join. It's a cycle."

Many people think of fraternities as "drinking clubs," says Jonathan Brant, executive vice president of the 66-member National Interfraternity Conference. "We don't want to be perceived that way," he said. "The only way we will accomplish that is to substantially change our behavior." In December [1997], the conference unanimously approved a resolution encouraging member fraternities to maintain alcohol-free chapters.

An Increase in Alcohol-Free Fraternities

About 2,000 chapters reportedly have agreed to go substance free, which means they will not host parties with alcohol, nor allow alcohol in rooms.

[In 1997,] Phi Delta Theta and Sigma Nu became the first national fraternities to ban any drinking in fraternity houses, beginning in 2000. And many sorority houses have been dry for years. Lissa Bradford, president of the National Panhellenic Conference, says the organization's nearly 3,000 chapters do not allow alcohol in their chapter houses.

Four schools—Florida Southern College, Southern Illinois University at Carbondale, the University of Northern Colorado and Villanova—are testing a program [during the 1997–98 academic year] requiring all fraternity houses on campus to be "dry." But some fraternities at Southern Illinois balked at complying with the program, which was created by national fraternity leaders and college administrators.

National peer networks like BACCHUS (Boost Alcohol Consciousness Concerning the Health of University Students) and GAMMA (Greeks Advocating Mature Management of Alcohol) are also working with Greek houses to promote responsible attitudes toward alcohol.

Rich Zeolia, a senior at the University of Maryland and past president of the Phi Delta Theta chapter, says fraternities at Maryland must comply with university rules or forgo parties. The rules include checking IDs, party monitoring by sober fraternity members, no hard liquor and the posting of date-rape information and emergency hotline numbers. Zeolia says he made sure the rules were followed when he was president, but that, "In my opinion, the university is not strict enough. We are just one drink away from a tragedy here, like on other campuses. When there is alcohol poisoning or hazing, universities need to send a strong message."

"Learner Permits" for Underage Drinkers

Roderic B. Park, interviewed by David J. Hanson

In the following interview, Roderic B. Park tells David J. Hanson that issuing "learner permits" to underage drinkers could help reduce teenage alcohol abuse. Park explains that many of the problems caused by underage drinking are due to the fact that younger drinkers do not understand the consequences of alcohol abuse or know how to drink moderately. According to Park, these permits would help teenagers learn how to drink responsibly by providing educational programs and allowing them to drink under parental or guardian supervision. Park, the Senior Associate for Academic Development, University of California at Merced, is a former chancellor at the University of Colorado at Boulder. Hanson is a sociology professor at the State University of New York at Potsdam and the author of *Alcohol Education: What We Must Do.*

Dr. Hanson—

Dr. Park, you served as Chancellor of the University of Colorado as well as the Vice Chancellor at Berkeley and have had many years of experience with college students. Could you explain the problem of alcohol abuse among college students and other young people?

Dr. Park—

Yes. Currently, young people can legally purchase and drink alcohol only when they reach the arbitrary age of 21. There is no educational requirement before they can legally purchase, such as knowledge of legal limitations and liabilities, the facts of intoxication, or the role of intoxication in the transmission of sexually transmitted diseases. There is no reason to assume that people suddenly and magically become mature or wise or thoughtful at any arbitrary age. Nevertheless, in a kind of simplistic hypocrisy, the age of 21 law has become part of our culture's "solution" to the problem of irresponsible drinking. Indeed, if this law actually worked, and a decrease in automobile fatalities of ages 16–20 could be attributed to the age 21 law, why not make it age 25—or 34—or 42?

Reprinted from Roderic B. Park, interviewed by David J. Hanson, "Drinking 'Learner Permits' for Under-Age Persons," available at www2.potsdam.edu/alcoholinfo/InTheirOwnWords/ParkInterview.html. Reprinted with permission from David J. Hanson.

On the other hand, we permit people to marry, join the military, sign legally binding contracts, and vote at the age of 18. Thus a couple getting married at the age of 20 can't enjoy a toast of champagne at their wedding! Not very logical.

The Ill Effects of Current Legislation

Dr. Hanson—

I see your point. What are the effects of the current age 21 legislation?
Dr. Park—

Well, it is clear that the minimum drinking age of 21 is not working. Recent national surveys show that about 90% of U.S. high school students have consumed alcohol beverages. Half of these teenagers drink regularly. These are "inexperienced" drinkers who have generally received no education on the personal and social consequences of alcohol abuse and are typically acting without parental knowledge or guidance.

Such inexperienced and untutored young people usually consume alcohol in an environment with a lack of norms promoting moderation. We see the results daily in the police blotter. Lives are ruined or cut short, families are heart-broken, and society loses productive human resources. Police write endless citations in an almost futile effort to reduce underage drinking, which has the effect of driving it underground into even less social-controlled environments, making drinking abuse worse. And of course, underage drinking leads to a disrespect for law among young people, who see the legislation as unfair and discriminatory.

Underage drinking is also a concern of parents, many of whom have offered high school "keg parties" at home rather than accepting the alternative of young people out drinking and driving. Thus many parents are forced into joining the disregard for age 21 laws. We all join Mothers Against Drunk Driving (MADD) in our rejection of drunk driving. But if, as Benjamin Franklin stated, death and taxes are a certainty, so too are alcohol and automobiles. There is evidence that underage drinkers are more conscious than their parents about using designated non-drinking drivers. Why not build on this sense of responsibility among the young through a program of education and monitoring?

Allow Limited Underage Drinking

Dr. Hanson—

That's an intriguing concept. Could you elaborate on what you have in mind?

Dr. Park—

I think we should step up to the challenge of changing the youth culture from one that is too accepting of abusive behavior to one intolerant of abuse and promoting responsibility. We should consider establishing a type of "learner's permit" for limited alcohol consumption, similar in concept to the driver's permit. With parental or guardian permission, a person under the age of 21 might apply for such a "license" which allowed limited use of beverage alcohol under monitored conditions where the licensee is held accountable. Licensing would occur within the context of educational programs and parental or guardian supervision. Permit cards, similar to a student driving license, could be issued for the purchase of alcohol and, like a driving license, could serve as a social contract used to help monitor the holder's conduct.

One prerequisite for receiving the card would be passing a course on the expectations of responsible use of alcohol, what constitutes acceptable and unacceptable conduct, and the consequences of alcohol abuse. We have similar, clearly defined expectations for receiving a driver's license; why not have the same for alcohol consumption?

Dr. Hanson—

This seems like a positive rather than negative approach to the problem, doesn't it?

Dr. Park—

Yes. I have always believed that the way people become most responsible is by giving them responsibility. I think young adults would be responsible with such a privilege following education and with appropriate monitoring. Federal legislation allowing states to experiment within certain guidelines and with careful monitoring would lead us to more civil, productive and effective citizenship for our sons and daughters.

Possible Problems with Drinking Licenses

Dr. Hanson—

Are there any potential downsides from this approach?

Dr. Park—

Well, first, we would be trying to change an "alcohol culture" and that could be difficult. However, I am encouraged by such an effort at the University of Colorado at Boulder. During the first year of our programs police reports of alcohol-related incidents around football games were running at less than half the previous level. Fraternities and sororities are running dry formal events. We received support from local police, from the Parents Association and from the Commissioner of the Big XII Conference representing the Big XII presidents.

Dr. Hanson—

Well, MADD and Students Against Destructive Decisions (SADD) had remarkable success in changing our society's drunk driving attitudes and behaviors. . . . and they did so in a short period, so I think you have good reason to be very optimistic. Are there any other potential problems?

Dr. Park—

Some in the advertising industry might try to exploit a new and younger population. However others are promoting and engaging in responsible advertising, a trend which should be encouraged. Could education and monitoring outweigh these two potential risks? I believe they would. I have confidence that our young people will be more responsible when properly educated and given appropriate responsibility with guidance and positive societal expectations.

No one can be certain that any particular idea such as the "learner's permit" will work. The point is to seek creative and workable solutions to the tragic consequences of alcohol abuse in American society. We can and must do better.

Dr. Hanson—

Thank you very much for sharing your thoughts with us.

DO NOT LOWER THE DRINKING AGE

Alcohol Policies Project

Age-21 laws set the legal drinking age in the United States at twenty-one. Some people want to lower the age, typically to eighteen, which was the legal drinking age for much of the nation until the 1980s. In the following selection, the Alcohol Policies Project responds to specific arguments for ending age-21 laws and contends that lowering the drinking age will worsen the problem of teenage alcoholism. The project asserts that laws that require a person be at least twenty-one years old in order to purchase or consume alcohol have helped decrease alcohol consumption among teenagers. It states that lowering the drinking age to eighteen will lead to more opportunities for younger teens to drink and will not encourage responsible drinking. The Alcohol Policies Project, an offshoot of the Center for Science in the Public Interest, focuses attention on policy reforms that will help reduce the health and social consequences of drinking.

State Age-21 laws are one of the most effective public policies ever implemented in the Nation . . . I am chagrined to report that some supposedly responsible officials would like to repeal them.

Jim Hall, Chairman
National Transportation Safety Board

Argument
Lowering the drinking age will reduce the allure of alcohol as a "forbidden fruit" for minors.

Response
Lowering the drinking age will make alcohol more available to an even younger population, replacing "forbidden fruit" with "low-hanging fruit."

The practices and behaviors of 18 year-olds are particularly influential on 15–17 year-olds. If 18 year-olds get the OK to drink, they will be modeling drinking for younger teens. Legal access to alcohol for 18 year-olds will provide more opportunities for younger teens to obtain it illegally from older peers.

Age-21 has resulted in decreases, not increases in youth drinking,

Reprinted from Alcohol Policies Project, "Talking Points/Arguments: Answering the Critics of Age-21," available at www.cspinet.org/booze/mlpatalk.htm. Reprinted with permission from the Center for Science in the Public Interest.

an outcome inconsistent with an increased allure of alcohol. In 1983, one year before the National Minimum Purchase Age Act was passed, 88% of high school seniors reported any alcohol use in the past year and 41% reported binge drinking. By 1997, alcohol use by seniors had dropped to 75% and the percentage of binge drinkers had fallen to 31%.

Lowering the Drinking Age Will Not Increase Responsibility

Argument

Lowering the drinking age will encourage young people to be responsible consumers. They'll get an idea of their tolerance and learn to drink under supervision at bars (or on campus, if in college), rather than at uncontrolled private parties away from school.

Response

No evidence exists to indicate that kids will learn to drink responsibly simply because they are able to consume alcohol legally at a younger age. Countries with lower drinking ages suffer from alcohol-related problems similar to those in the U.S.

Responsible consumption comes with maturity, and maturity largely comes as certain protective mechanisms, such as marriage and first job, begin to take hold.

Supervision does not necessarily lead to responsibility. Many bars encourage irresponsible drinking by deeply discounting drinks and by heavily promoting specials, such as happy hours, two-for-ones, and bar crawls.

Raising the drinking age has apparently increased responsibility among young people. Compared to 1980 when less than 21 was the norm, fewer college students in 1995 reported drinking in the past month (68% vs. 82%) and binge drinking (39% vs. 44%). Also, more college students disapproved of binge drinking (66% vs. 57%).

The 1978 *National Study of Adolescent Drinking Behavior* found that 10th–12th graders in states with lower drinking ages drank significantly more, were drunk more often, and were less likely to abstain from alcohol. Additionally, national data show that high school seniors who could not legally drink until age 21 drank less before age 21 and between ages 21–25 than did students in states with lower drinking ages.

Age-21 Laws Are Effective

Argument

At 18, kids can vote, join the military, sign contracts, and even smoke. Why shouldn't they be able to drink?

Response

Ages of initiation vary—One may vote at 18, drink at 21, rent a car at 25, and run for president at 35. These ages may appear arbitrary, but they take into account the requirements, risks, and benefits of each act.

When age-21 was challenged in Louisiana's State Supreme Court, the Court upheld the law, ruling that ". . . statutes establishing the minimum drinking age at a higher level than the age of majority are not arbitrary because they substantially further the appropriate governmental purpose of improving highway safety, and thus are constitutional."

Age-21 laws help keep kids healthy by postponing the onset of alcohol use. Deferred drinking reduces the risks of:
- developing alcohol dependence or abuse later in life.
- harming the developing brain.
- engaging in current and adult drug use.
- suffering alcohol-related problems, such as trouble at work, with friends, family, and police.

Argument

Minors still drink, so age-21 laws clearly don't work.

Response

Age-21 laws work. Young people drink less in response. The laws have saved an estimated 17,000 lives since states began implementing them in 1975, and they've decreased the number of alcohol-related youth fatalities among drivers by 63% since 1982.

Stricter enforcement of age-21 laws against commercial sellers would make those laws even more effective at reducing youth access to alcohol. The ease with which young people acquire alcohol—three-quarters of 8th graders say that it is "fairly easy" or "very easy" to get—indicates that more must be done. Current laws against sales to minors need stiff penalties to deter violations. Better education and prevention-oriented laws are needed to reduce the commercial pressures on kids to drink.

WHY I TELL MY TEENAGE PATIENTS TO DRINK

Patricia J. Roy

In the following selection, Patricia J. Roy, a doctor, explains why she believes that teenage alcoholism can be lessened if parents allow their teenagers to drink at home. Roy argues that teenagers are better off if they learn to drink at family dinners rather than at parties. According to Roy, children of alcoholics can learn about drinking from other responsible adults.

It's true: I tell my teenage patients to drink. In fact, I strongly encourage it. Is my advice illegal? Some may say so. Controversial? No doubt. Will it save lives? Absolutely.

A New Approach

After I'd been in practice for about five years, I realized that I'd lost one teenage patient to a drunken-driving accident annually. I was certain there had to be a way to prevent such needless deaths, and I vowed to try. But first I had to examine what motivates kids to drink.

Obviously, peer pressure plays a large role in teenage drinking, as does the excitement of doing something rebellious and illegal. But what if the thrill were removed and drinking were to become ordinary—as it is in Italy and France, where teens routinely drink wine with meals? And what if American parents actually taught their kids how to drink responsibly?

The more I mulled over those questions, the more sense it made to stop treating teenage drinking as a taboo. So I decided to revise the talk I give teens when they come in with their parents for health-maintenance exams.

My 25-minute speech—which covers smoking, drinking, drugs, and sex—has earned a bit of a reputation. When I tell teenage patients they'll have to suffer through it, they say they've heard about it, and roll their eyes in mock dread. And often the parent will add, "I was hoping you'd give it."

I start with the perils of smoking. "It's a choice only you can make," I say, "but I hope you'll decide not to smoke." Then I segue into alcohol. "While you may never smoke," I say, "it's doubtful that

Excerpted from Patricia J. Roy, "Teenage Patients: Tell Them to Drink," *Medical Economics*, March 10, 1997. Reprinted with permission from *Medical Economics*.

you'll never touch alcohol during your life." Parents who are prepared for a just-say-No lecture jerk to attention at this point. The teens usually grin. Then I ask whether the family has any religious or philosophical reasons to abstain from alcohol. If the answer is Yes, and the teen plans to adhere to the no-drinking policy, I commend his or her healthy choice and move on to the next point.

But most of my teenage patients live in homes where beer, wine, and hard liquor are present. So I say to the parent, "You may not agree with this, but as long as you have alcohol in the house, I highly recommend that you let your kid have some."

"Yes!!!" say the boys, without exception. The girls smile coyly. The parents usually look shocked.

"Listen, we're being incredibly naive as parents if we think our teenagers will wait until they're 21 to have their first drink," I say. Even the strictest parents nod in agreement. "If your family is having pizza at home on a Friday night, and the adults are having beer, give some to your kids if they want it. Or a glass of wine. Or a wine cooler.

"Drinking is a social skill that must be taught, like table manners. Kids should learn how to drink responsibly under the guidance of someone who cares and won't let anything happen to them."

Learning from Adults

Then I look at my teen patient and say, "The place to find out that your limit is three beers is at home, in your parents' presence—not at your friend's party or, worse, when you're behind the wheel of a car." I tell them about my teen patients who were killed in drunken-driving accidents. "A couple of them," I say, "were sober but dumb enough to get in the car with someone who wasn't. If you go to a party, you don't have to drink, because you can do that at home. Teens who opt not to drink at parties tell me their friends are jealous of them because they're permitted to drink at home. Their friends also are happy to have a designated driver."

If parents want to ignore my advice, I tell them that's fine. But I want them to discuss the issue with their kids and make a decision together—instead of closing their eyes to teenage drinking. "The worst that will happen is you'll have a very interesting dinner conversation tonight," I tell them.

Naturally, I amend my approach for families that have problem drinkers. If the parents are alcoholics, as their family doctor, I often know it. And if I don't, I ask the teens privately whether Mom or Dad has a drinking problem. They always know, and my question gives them the opportunity to talk about it in a non-threatening environment. I've referred several children to Alateen, and I've sent a couple to Alcoholics Anonymous after they've confided that they have a drinking problem.

I tell teens who have an alcoholic parent that problem drinking often runs in families, as an inherited tendency and a learned behavior. But rather than tell the kids not to touch alcohol, I explain the signs of alcoholism—then encourage them to learn responsible drinking from a levelheaded adult.

Treating Teens with Respect

Whether I'm talking to teens about drugs, smoking, sex, or alcohol, I always acknowledge their ability and right to make choices. But I stress that, if they're adult enough to make decisions, they must be adult enough to suffer the consequences. . . .

Besides telling teens what they need to know, my frank words also establish a deeper trust between us. They know I'll treat them with respect and won't betray their confidences. Consequently, I've had kids tell me about their bulimia, sexual activity, and, most recently, a suicide attempt.

Since I've been advising my teen patients to drink at home, none has died in a drunken-driving accident. I can't claim credit for that, but I do like to think I'm helping to provide the community with a group of teenage designated drivers who get their friends home from parties safely. And I'm hopeful they'll grow into adults who'll drink responsibly and teach their own kids to do the same.

Changing Permissive Attitudes Toward Teenage Drinking

Anne M. Weeks

Anne M. Weeks writes that in order for the problem of teenage alcohol abuse to decrease, parents and the media need to end their permissive attitudes toward teenage drinking. Many parents either encourage or ignore their children's drinking, she notes, sometimes with fatal consequences. Weeks also contends that television programs make underage drinking seem appealing. She concludes that parents and educators must send a clear message to teenagers that drinking is unacceptable. Weeks is an English teacher and the director of college guidance at the Old-fields School in Glencoe, Maryland.

The whole issue of excessive drinking on college campuses has been on my mind a lot lately, partly due to my experiences as a college guidance counselor, but also because I have a son who has just entered high school and will be facing this rite of passage all too soon. As a college counselor in a private boarding school, I am responsible for preparing and guiding our students in the college-application process, but as is typical of boarding schools, I also take a great interest in how our students fare once they are enrolled in the colleges of their choice.

Few Nonalcoholic Activities

In recent years, I have found a small but vocal group of graduates who complain that the social scene on their respective campuses provides little that is not alcohol-related. They encounter students who have discovered their first taste of freedom, often translated into setting up extensive bars in their rooms, or demonstrated through spending the majority of their time seeking social situations that revolve around alcohol use. In each case, I ask what entertainment the college is providing for those who choose to abstain, and the answer, more often than not, is that "there are great programs with magicians, hypnotists, and comedians, even coffeehouses, but they all wind down around 10:00 P.M., and then what is there to do?"

Excerpted from Anne M. Weeks, "Who's Serving?" *Education Week*, July 12, 2000. Reprinted with permission from the author.

Even those students who happily join in with the drinking gang often discover after one semester that this behavior has directly affected their academic performance, and when they choose to limit their involvement, they find they are socially bored. As a result, I see a growing trend of students who want to live off campus in their own apartments, where they can create a more adult lifestyle and avoid the immature behavior they perceive to be rampant in college dormitories.

This past fall, I came to realize that one small, liberal arts college in particular had a high rate of transfer among our graduates. When I have questioned these former students about their dissatisfactions with the college, it always came back to the same problem: social alcohol use, or should I say, abuse, among their classmates. When speaking with my colleagues in our local private schools, I found they had uncovered a similar dissatisfaction among their graduates with this college. What I found most striking, however, is that this college had instituted a very strict policy on alcohol use two years ago, and as far as I was able to ascertain, was following through on its stated guidelines with tenacious consistency. So, why did students still want to transfer to extricate themselves from the social alcohol scene?

I decided the best way to research this issue was to ask the college's representative about it when she visited my school last fall. I have never been shy about trying to get an answer to a question I pose, so I jumped right in and grilled this young, perky representative, who I suspected was not used to a seasoned counselor putting her in the witness chair for cross-examination. What I anticipated was a vague answer that would include the usual "we have magicians, hypnotists, comedians, and even a coffeehouse" response, but was completely surprised, and frankly impressed, to receive a thoughtful, yet alarming, response. She told me that she felt the college was actually inheriting a problem when the students enrolled. Her observation was that students arrived at her college with an unhealthy attitude about drinking, well-established during their high school years, and as a result, the college was put in the position of having to combat a pre-existing problem. What an interesting perspective. Because she was a young representative who had recently graduated herself, I felt this perspective was well worth my consideration, and thus, the advent of my rumination on this topic.

Some Parents Encourage Drinking

Over the past few years, several alcohol-related events have caught my eye:

A senior throws a party for his friends. The parents allow alcohol to be served with the understanding that all drivers must turn in their car keys and spend the night. Later that night, their own son and a companion take the keys to the family car with the intention of picking up some girls.

The son, trying to negotiate a turn, hits a utility pole and is instantly killed, while his companion is thrown from the car and sustains permanent injury. The parents of the deceased place a memorial plaque in the student's school that includes a photo of the son with a beer in his hand.

Merely two weeks later, parents from the same school host another alcohol-related event at their home, shuttling the kids out to their house from a common parking spot.

A middle schooler throws a party for his friends. The parents are home and are monitoring the party from the second floor of the house. A 12-year-old drinks an excessive number of shots of hard liquor, and when the others cannot awaken him, they alert the parents. The child spends two days in the hospital recovering from severe alcohol poisoning.

The police bust up a party on the fields of a local college, only to find that a majority of the students are underage, local high school students.

This, it seems, had been a favored Friday-night party spot for some time.

When a local school discovers that a number of its students have been involved and addresses the parents with concern, phone calls flood in from parents angry at the school's response. It becomes evident that parents had actually helped provide alcohol and knowingly dropped their children off at the field for the evening.

A neighbor hires a housesitter for her 14-year-old son for a Saturday night. She allows the son to invite a friend to spend the night. The friend is driven to the house by a parent. He arrives already under the influence of alcohol, and somehow, after the parent leaves, there is also a box with two cases of beer in the drive. Other friends arrive, and the housesitter becomes alarmed. The friends are sent home, and when the neighbor calls the parents the following morning, she gets little cooperation in determining how to address the issue of underage drinking among these boys. The parents do not want to discuss it and openly admit that they have not only failed to discuss the incident with their sons, but have not punished them.

In order to sneak alcohol into a 7th grade dance, boys melt the bottoms of plastic straws and fill them with hard alcohol, carrying as many as 20 straws in their pockets.

At a middle school's parent-student alcohol- and drug-discussion night, two parents argue about the correct way to handle the knowledge of one of their son's potential substance abuse. One parent says he would want to have the other parent notify him if that parent observed or had knowledge of a problem with his son. The other parent responds by saying he would never want to be notified, that it was his business what his son did and no one else's. The two men have known each other since childhood and are business colleagues.

I could cite examples such as these unendingly, as could most high school counselors and teachers. But is it just ineffective parenting that is to blame? I think not.

Television Encourages Teenage Alcohol Abuse

In the past year and a half, I have had a group of students come to my home every Wednesday night to watch the popular television program *Dawson's Creek*. Though I am well beyond the age of enjoying a teenage soap opera, this show caught my attention with its unique format. There is a high quality of moral and ethical lessons communicated on a regular basis on this show. It presents typical teenage problems and addresses them in a thoughtful manner. I have been further impressed by the extensive vocabulary the characters use, and I appreciate the show's ability to make the vocabulary work well within the dialogue and thus to expose teenagers to new words.

However, even in this show, clearly designed to be the other extreme from *Beverly Hills 90210* in its presentation of teens' lives, there are messages, both blatant and subtle, that suggest to the teenage audience that underage drinking is acceptable.

[In the 1999–2000 season,] the characters were seen spending an evening at a local nightclub, where they were not carded and were served mixed drinks, despite being only 15 years old. This season, the title character wallowed in his sorrows at a strip joint, where he not only was served alcohol, but also met a stripper who turned out to be 16 years old. When the characters are seen drinking sodas, they are often drinking root beer in brown bottles that look suspiciously like beer bottles. What message is this sending? When a majority of the students watching this show are given the impression that it will provide them with wholesome role models, why would they not assume that this attitude toward underage drinking is acceptable, indeed encouraged?

Attitudes Must Be Changed

All of this brings me to only one conclusion. In the recent atmosphere of blame leveled at colleges for not controlling abusive drinking habits, maybe we are focusing our concern and angst toward the wrong constituency. Maybe we should be looking more carefully at the attitudes of parents and the media when guiding and nurturing our children in their formative years. Maybe we should face the fact that colleges cannot effectively be in loco parentis and should not be expected to be.

Let us start seriously addressing the alcohol problem in the teenage years and discover how we can effectively, as parents and educators, raise responsible children with responsible attitudes. Let us stop giving credence to peer pressure and face the fact that we, as adults, are not successfully creating an environment that frowns upon the abuse of alcohol.

REDUCING DRINKING AND DRIVING BY YOUNG DRIVERS

National Highway Traffic Safety Administration

In the following article, the National Highway Traffic Safety Administration (NHTSA) explains how zero-tolerance laws have reduced drinking and driving among younger drivers. Such laws make it illegal for a person under the age of twenty-one to drive with a blood alcohol level greater than .02. According to the NHTSA, these laws have reduced alcohol-related crashes among younger drivers by as much as 16 percent.

The U.S. Department of Transportation's National Highway Traffic Safety Administration (NHTSA) encourages States to enact zero-tolerance laws designed to reduce drinking and driving among younger drivers. Such laws should:

• establish that any measurable amount (a maximum of .02) of alcohol in the blood, breath, or urine of a driver under age 21 would be an "illegal per se" offense; and

• provide for immediate driver's license suspension periods for those under age 21 who exceed the applicable blood-alcohol concentration (BAC) limit.

Laws Against Underage Drinking

All 50 States and the District of Columbia now have laws that prohibit the purchase and public possession of alcoholic beverages by those under the age of 21. Therefore, it would seem reasonable to expect drivers under the age of 21 to have no alcohol in their systems, and the appropriate BAC for these drivers would be zero.

However, for enforcement purposes, some States have enacted laws that establish a BAC level of .02, at which it is illegal for those under the age of 21 to operate a motor vehicle. NHTSA supports those laws.

Younger drivers place a high value on their drivers' licenses, and the threat of license revocation has proved to be an especially effective sanction for this age group.

Thirty-seven States and the District of Columbia have set the BAC limit at .02 or lower for drivers under age 21: Alabama, Alaska, Arizona, Arkansas, California, Connecticut, Delaware, District of Colum-

Excerpted from the National Highway Traffic Safety Administration, U.S. Department of Transportation, "Zero-Tolerance Laws to Reduce Alcohol-Impaired Driving by Youth."

bia, Florida, Idaho, Illinois, Indiana, Iowa, Kansas, Kentucky, Maine, Maryland, Massachusetts, Michigan, Minnesota, Missouri, Montana, Nebraska, New Hampshire, New Jersey, New Mexico, New York, North Carolina, Ohio, Oklahoma, Oregon, Pennsylvania, Rhode Island, Tennessee, Utah, Virginia, Washington, and West Virginia. To correspond to age 21 alcohol purchase laws, NHTSA supports the use of age 21 as an appropriate threshold for lower BAC limits and longer suspension periods.

Typically, zero-tolerance laws provide that any amount of alcohol in the body of a driver under age 21 (generally measured as .02 percent BAC or greater) is an offense for which the driver's license may be suspended. These laws should allow a police officer to require a breath test from any driver under the age of 21 if the officer has probable cause to believe that the individual has been drinking (and should not require that the officer have a probable cause to suspect actual impairment). Refusal to take such a test should result in license suspension under implied consent or administrative license revocation laws.

Zero-Tolerance Laws Work

Several studies show conclusively that zero-tolerance laws save lives. For example:

• Maryland's zero-tolerance law produced an 11 percent decrease in drinking drivers under age 21 involved in crashes.

• In a study of four other States, fatal crashes at night involving young drivers dropped by 8 percent more than in comparison States after zero-tolerance laws were adopted.

• A recent study compared fatal crashes in 12 States that enacted zero-tolerance laws for some young drivers to crashes in 12 nearby States without these laws. In the 12 zero-tolerance States, single vehicle nighttime fatal crashes involving young drivers dropped 16 percent, while in the comparison States they rose 1 percent.

Making any amount of alcohol in the body of an underage person an offense can make the enforcement effort easier. If the officer has any reason to suspect that the individual has been drinking, he or she can demand a breath test and take action to arrest the underage driver. Passive sensors, which can detect low BACs, permit the police to identify individuals with small amounts of alcohol in their bodies. This has the potential to reduce enforcement and adjudication time and expense, particularly if handled in an administrative process.

Penalties Faced by States

States that do not consider a .02 BAC (or less) to be driving while intoxicated for drivers under age 21 will be subject to the withholding of Federal-Aid Highway funds beginning in Fiscal Year 1999. To comply with the Federal law, State laws must:

• apply to all persons under the age of 21;

- set .02 BAC or less as the legal limit;
- establish .02 as a "per se" offense (without having to prove intoxication);
- provide for primary enforcement; and
- provide that license suspensions or revocations are authorized as sanctions for any violation of the State zero-tolerance law.

SENSIBLE DRINKING MESSAGES WILL END ALCOHOL ABUSE

Stanton Peele and Archie Brodsky

In the following article, Stanton Peele and Archie Brodsky assert that present-day alcohol education teaches wrongly that any level of alcohol consumption can be considered alcohol abuse. The authors contend that American culture needs to turn away from its "temperance" attitudes—disapproving of drinking and encouraging alcohol abstinence—and instead provide teenagers with sensible messages about drinking. Parents and schools should teach adolescents that drinking does not cause violence and that positive drinking habits can be developed, Peele and Brodsky argue. Peele is the author of many books on alcohol and is a consultant for the International Center for Alcohol Policies, Washington, D.C., and the Wine Institute in San Francisco. Brodsky is a research associate in psychiatry at the Massachusetts Mental Health Center Program in Psychiatry and Law in Boston.

We in the United States have ample positive models of drinking to emulate, both in our own country and around the world. We have all the more reason to do so now that the federal government has revised its *Dietary Guidelines for Americans* to reflect the finding that alcohol has substantial health benefits. Beyond such official pronouncements, there are at least two crucial contact points to reach people with accurate and useful instruction about drinking.

Positive Socialization

We can best prepare young people to live in a world (and a nation) where most people do drink by teaching them the difference between responsible and irresponsible drinking. The most reliable mechanism for doing this is the positive parental model. Indeed, the single most crucial source of constructive alcohol education is the family that puts drinking in perspective, using it to enhance social gatherings in which people of all ages and both genders participate. (Picture the dif-

Excerpted from Stanton Peele and Archie Brodsky, "The Antidote to Alcohol Abuse: Sensible Drinking Messages," in *Wine in Context: Nutrition, Physiology, Policy: Proceedings of the Symposium on Wine & Health, 24 & 25 June 1996* (Davis, CA: American Society for Enology and Viticulture, 1996), edited by Andrew L. Waterhouse and JoAnne M. Rantz. Reprinted with permission from JoAnne M. Rantz.

ference between drinking with your family and drinking with "the boys.") Alcohol does not drive the parents' behavior: it doesn't keep them from being productive, and it doesn't make them aggressive and violent. By this example, children learn that alcohol need not disrupt their lives or serve as an excuse for violating normal social standards.

Ideally, this positive modeling at home would be reinforced by sensible-drinking messages in school. Unfortunately, in today's neo-temperance times, alcohol education in school is dominated by a prohibitionist hysteria that cannot acknowledge positive drinking habits. As with illicit drugs, all alcohol use is classified as misuse. A child who comes from a family in which alcohol is drunk in a convivial and sensible manner is thus bombarded by exclusively negative information about alcohol. Although children may parrot this message in school, such an unrealistic alcohol education is drowned out in high-school and college peer groups, where destructive binge-drinking has become the norm.

To illustrate this process with one ludicrous example, a high-school newsletter for entering freshmen told its youthful readers that a person who begins to drink at age 13 has an 80 percent chance of becoming an alcoholic! It added that the average age at which children begin to drink is 12. Does that mean that nearly half of today's children will grow up to be alcoholic? Is it any wonder that high-school and college students cynically dismiss these warnings? It seems as though schools want to tell children as many negative things as possible about alcohol, whether or not they stand any chance of being believed.

Recent research has found that antidrug programs like Drug Abuse Resistance Education (DARE) are not effective. Dennis Gorman, the Director of Prevention Research at the Rutgers Center of Alcohol Studies, believes this is due to the failure of such programs to address the community milieu where alcohol and drug use occurs. It is especially self-defeating to have the school program and family and community values in conflict. Think of the confusion when a child returns from school to a moderate-drinking home to call a parent who is drinking a glass of wine a "drug abuser." Often the child is relaying messages from Alcoholics Anonymous (AA) members who lecture school children about the dangers of alcohol. In this case, the blind (uncontrolled drinkers) are leading the sighted (moderate drinkers). This is wrong, scientifically and morally, and counterproductive for individuals, families, and society.

Intervention Is Effective

Along with bringing up our children in an atmosphere that encourages moderate drinking, it would be useful to have a nonintrusive way to help adults monitor their consumption patterns, i.e., to provide a periodic check on a habit that, for some, can get out of hand. Such a corrective mechanism is available in the form of brief interventions by physicians. Brief interventions can substitute for, and have been found superior to, specialized alcohol-abuse treatments. In the course of a physical examination or other clinical visit, the physician (or other health professional) asks about the patient's drinking and, if necessary, advises the patient to change the behavior in question so as to reduce the health risks involved.

Medical research worldwide shows that brief intervention is as effective and cost-effective a treatment as we have for alcohol abuse. Yet so extreme is the ideological bias against any alcohol consumption in the U.S. that physicians are afraid to advise patients about safe levels of drinking. While European physicians routinely dispense such advice, physicians in this country hesitate even to suggest that patients reduce their consumption, for fear of implying that some level of drinking can be positively recommended. In an article in a prominent U.S. medical journal, Dr. Katharine Bradley and her colleagues urge physicians to adopt this technique. They write: "There is no evidence from studies of heavy drinkers in Britain, Sweden, and Norway that alcohol consumption increases when heavy drinkers are advised to drink less; in fact it decreases."

So much for the fear that people cannot be trusted to hear balanced, medically sound information about the effects of alcohol.

Creating a Culture of Moderation

In the uneasy mix of ethnic drinking cultures that we call the United States of America, we see the bifurcation characteristic of a temperance culture, with a large number of abstainers (30%) and small but still troubling minorities of alcohol-dependent drinkers (5%) and nondependent problem drinkers (15%) among the adult population. Even so, we have a large culture of moderation, with the largest category (50%) of adult Americans being social, nonproblem drinkers. Most Americans who drink do so in a responsible manner. The typical wine drinker generally consumes 2 or fewer glasses on any given occasion, usually at mealtimes and in the company of family or friends.

And yet, still driven by the demons of the Temperance movement, we are doing our best to destroy that positive culture by ignoring or denying its existence. Writing in *American Psychologist*, Stanton Peele noted with concern that "the attitudes that characterize both ethnic groups and individuals with the greatest drinking problems are being propagated as a national outlook." He went on to explain that "a range of cultural forces in our society has endangered the attitudes that underlie the norm and the practice of moderate drinking. The widespread propagation of the image of the irresistible dangers of alcohol has contributed to this undermining."

Selden Bacon, a founder and longtime director of what became the Rutgers Center of Alcohol Studies, has graphically described the perverse negativism of alcohol "education" in the U.S.:

> Current organized knowledge about alcohol use can be likened to . . . knowledge about automobiles and their use if the latter were limited to facts and theories about accidents and crashes. . . . [What is missing are] the positive functions and positive attitudes about alcohol uses in our as well as in other societies. . . . If educating youth about drinking starts from the assumed basis that such drinking is bad [and] . . . full of risk for life and property, at best considered as an escape, clearly useless per se, and/or frequently the precursor of disease, and the subject matter is taught by nondrinkers and antidrinkers, this is a particular indoctrination. Further, if 75–80% of the surrounding peers and elders are or are going to become drinkers, there [is] . . . an inconsistency between the message and the reality.

What is the result of this negative indoctrination? During the past few decades per capita alcohol consumption in the U.S. has declined, yet the number of problem drinkers (according to clinical and self-identification) continues to rise, especially in younger age groups. This frustrating trend contradicts the notion that reducing the overall consumption of alcohol—by restricting availability or raising prices—will result in fewer alcohol problems, even though this panacea is widely promoted in the public-health field. Doing something meaningful about alcohol abuse requires a more profound intervention than "sin taxes" and restricted hours of operation; it requires cultural and attitudinal changes.

We can do better than we are; after all, we once did do better. In eighteenth-century America, when drinking took place more in a communal context than it does now, per capita consumption was 2–3 times current levels, but drinking problems were rare and loss of control was absent from contemporary descriptions of drunkenness. Let's see if we can recover the poise, balance, and good sense our founding fathers and mothers showed in dealing with alcohol.

It is long past time to tell the American people the truth about alcohol, instead of a destructive fantasy that too often becomes a self-fulfilling prophecy. Revising the *Dietary Guidelines for Americans* is a necessary, but not sufficient condition for transforming a culture of abstinence warring with excess into a culture of moderate, responsible, healthy drinking.

ORGANIZATIONS TO CONTACT

The editors have compiled the following list of organizations concerned with the issues debated in this book. Descriptions are derived from materials provided by the organizations. All have publications or information available for interested readers. The list was compiled on the date of publication of the present volume; names, addresses, phone and fax numbers, and e-mail/Internet addresses may change. Be aware that many organizations take several weeks or longer to respond to inquiries, so allow as much time as possible.

Al-Anon Family Groups Headquarters
1600 Corporate Landing Parkway, Virginia Beach, VA 23454-5617
(757) 563-1600 • fax: (757) 563-1655
e-mail: WSO@alanon.org • website: www.al-anon.alateen.org

Al-Anon is a fellowship of men, women, and children whose lives have been affected by an alcoholic family member or friend. Alateen consists primarily of teenaged Al-Anon members who hold meetings in order to share experiences and learn how to deal with the effects of another person's drinking. Al-Anon/Alateen publications include several books, the monthly magazine *The Forum*, the semiannual *Al-Anon Speaks Out*, the bimonthly *Alateen Talk*, and pamphlets, such as *To the Mother and Father of an Alcoholic, Dear Mom & Dad*, and *Alcoholism, the Family Disease*.

Alcoholics Anonymous (AA)
Grand Central Station, PO Box 459, New York, NY 10163
(212) 870-3400 • fax: (212) 870-3003
website: www.aa.org

Alcoholics Anonymous is a worldwide fellowship of sober alcoholics, whose recovery is based on Twelve Steps. AA requires no dues or fees and accepts no outside funds. It is self-supporting through voluntary contributions of members. It is not affiliated with any other organization. AA's primary purpose is to carry the AA message to the alcoholic who still suffers. Its publications include the pamphlets *A Brief Guide to Alcoholics Anonymous, Young People and AA*, and *A Message to Teenagers . . . How to Tell When Drinking Is Becoming a Problem*.

The Beer Institute
122 C St. NW, Suite 750, Washington, DC 20001-2150
(202) 737-2337
e-mail: info@beerinstitute.org • website: www.beerinst.org

The Beer Institute is the official trade association for the American brewing industry. It promotes drinking in moderation and has implemented programs such as alcohol awareness curricula in schools and public service announcements to combat underage drinking and drunk driving. *Focus on Underage Drinking* and *Guarding Against Drug and Alcohol Abuse in the Nineties* are among its many publications.

Canadian Centre on Substance Abuse (CCSA)
75 Albert St., Suite 300, Ottawa ON K1P 5E7 Canada
(613) 235-4048 ext. 222 • fax: (613) 235-8108
e-mail: info@ccsa.ca • website: www.ccsa.ca

The CCSA is a Canadian clearinghouse on substance abuse. It works to disseminate information on the nature, extent, and consequences of substance abuse and to support and assist organizations involved in substance abuse treatment, prevention, and educational programming. The CCSA publishes reports, policy documents, brochures, research papers, the newsletter *Action News*, and several books, including *Canadian Profile: Alcohol, Tobacco, and Other Drugs*. Its website provides resources and information on youth drinking.

Center for Science in the Public Interest (CSPI)—Alcohol Policies Project
1875 Connecticut Ave. NW, Suite 300, Washington, DC 20009
(202) 332-9110 • fax: (202) 265-4954
e-mail: cspi@cspinet.org • website: www.cspinet.org/booze

CSPI launched the Alcohol Policies Project to reduce the devastating health and social consequences of drinking. The project's prevention-oriented policy strategy is aimed at curbing alcohol-related problems by advocating advertising reforms, increased excise taxes, and expanded warning requirements. Its publications include the quarterly newsletter *BoozeNews*, fact sheets on topics such as binge drinking and alcohol advertising, and the report *Last Call for High-Risk Bar Promotions That Target College Students*.

Distilled Spirits Council of the United States (DISCUS)
1250 Eye St. NW, Suite 400, Washington, DC 20005
(202) 628-3544 • fax: (202) 682-8888
website: www.discus.health.org

The Distilled Spirits Council of the United States is the national trade association representing producers and marketers of distilled spirits sold in the United States. It seeks to ensure the responsible advertising and marketing of distilled spirits to adult consumers and to prevent such advertising and marketing from targeting individuals below the legal purchase age. DISCUS fact sheets and pamphlets, including *The Drunk Driving Prevention Act*, are available at its website.

Mothers Against Drunk Driving (MADD)
511 E. John Carpenter Frwy., #700, Irving, TX 75062
(800) 438-6233
e-mail: info@madd.org • website: www.madd.org

Mothers Against Drunk Driving seeks to act as the voice of victims of drunk driving accidents by speaking on their behalf to communities, businesses, and educational groups and by providing materials for use in medical facilities and health and driver education programs. Its website's "Under 21" section provides information for teens about alcohol and drunk driving. MADD publishes brochures, the newsletter *MADD in Action*, and *Driven* magazine.

National Association for Children of Alcoholics (NACoA)
11426 Rockville Pike, Suite 100, Rockville, MD 20852
(888) 554-COAS (554-2627) • fax: (301) 468-0987
e-mail: nacoa@erols.com • website: www.health.org/nacoa

NACoA is the only national nonprofit membership organization working on behalf of children of alcoholics. Its mission is to advocate for all children and families affected by alcoholism and other drug dependencies.

The association publishes books, pamphlets, videos, educational kits, and the bimonthly *NACoA Network Newsletter*.

National Center on Addiction and Substance Abuse (CASA)
Columbia University, 152 West 57th St., New York, NY 10019
(212) 841-5200 • fax: (212) 956-8020
website: www.casacolumbia.org

The National Center on Addiction and Substance Abuse brings together all professional disciplines needed to study and combat substance abuse, including alcohol abuse. CASA assesses what works in prevention, treatment, and law enforcement; informs Americans about the economic and social costs of substance abuse; and removes the stigma of substance abuse. Publications include the reports *Substance Abuse and the American Adolescent: A Report by the Commission on Substance Abuse Among America's Adolescents* and *Dangerous Liaisons: Substance Abuse and Sex*.

The National Clearinghouse for Alcohol and Drug Information (NCADI)
P.O. Box 2345, Rockville, MD 20847-2345
(800) 729-6686 • fax: (301) 468-6433
e-mail: info@health.org • website: www.health.org

The NCADI is the information service of the Center for Substance Abuse Prevention of the Substance Abuse and Mental Health Services Administration in the U.S. Department of Health & Human Services. NCADI is the world's largest resource for current information and materials concerning substance abuse. The organization distributes fact sheets, brochures, pamphlets, monographs, posters, and videotapes and provides prevention, intervention, and treatment resources to families, schools, and professionals. Its publications include *Patterns of Alcohol Use Among Adolescents and Associations with Emotional and Behavioral Problems, Alarming Costs of Youth Alcohol Abuse*, and *Tips for Teens About Alcohol*.

National Council on Alcoholism and Drug Dependence (NCADD)
12 West 21st St., New York, NY 10010
(212) 206-6770 • fax: (212) 645-1690
e-mail: national@ncadd.org • website: www.ncadd.org

NCADD is a volunteer health organization that helps individuals overcome addictions, develops substance abuse prevention and education programs for youth, and advises the federal government on drug and alcohol policies. It operates the Campaign to Prevent Kids From Drinking. Publications include fact sheets such as "Youth, Alcohol and Other Drugs," brochures, the quarterly newsletter *NCADD Amethyst*, and the monthly newsletter *NCADD Washington Report*.

National Institute on Alcohol Abuse and Alcoholism (NIAAA)
Willco Building, 6000 Executive Blvd., Bethesda, MD 20892-7003
(301) 496-4000
e-mail: niaaaweb-r@exchange.nih.gov • website: www.niaaa.nih.gov

NIAAA supports and conducts biomedical and behavioral research on the causes, consequences, treatment, and prevention of alcoholism and alcohol-related problems. Its College Drinking Initiative seeks to provide the NIAAA, policy makers, and college presidents with research on campus prevention and treatment programs. The NIAAA publishes the quarterly journal *Alcohol Research & Health* (formerly *Alcohol Health & Research World*), *Alcohol Alert* bulletins, pamphlets, and reports.

Rational Recovery
Box 800, Lotus, CA 95651
(530) 621-2667 • fax: (530) 622-4296
e-mail: icc@rational.org • website: www.rational.org/recovery

Rational Recovery is a national self-help organization that offers a cognitive rather than spiritual approach to recovery from alcoholism. Its philosophy holds that alcoholics can attain sobriety without depending on other people or a "higher power." It publishes materials about the organization and its use of rational-emotive therapy.

Students Against Destructive Decisions! (SADD)
SADD National, Box 800, Marlboro, MA 01752
(800) 787-5777 • fax: (508) 481-5759
website: www.saddonline.com

Also known as Students Against Driving Drunk, SADD's mission is to prevent underage drinking and drug use and to focus attention on the consequences of other decisions such as smoking, violence, and sexually transmitted diseases. SADD promotes a no-use message of alcohol and other drugs and encourages students not to participate in activities with destructive consequences. It publishes a newsletter, press releases, and also provides a "Contract for Life" that can be used to increase parent-child communication about alcohol and drug-related decisions.

The Wine Institute
425 Market St., Suite 1000, San Francisco, CA 94105
(415) 512-0151 • fax: (415) 442-0742
e-mail: communications@wineinstitute.org
website: www.wineinstitute.org

The Wine Institute introduces and advocates public policy measures to enhance the environment for the responsible consumption and enjoyment of wine. It publishes the monthly newsletter *Newsflash* and the reports "American Health Association Advisory Acknowledges 'Potentially Sizable Health Benefit' of Alcohol" and "Study Finds Better Brain Functioning Among Moderate Alcohol Consuming Women."

Internet Resources

Alcohol: Problems and Solutions Website
website: www2.potsdam.edu/alcohol-info

This website describes alcohol use and abuse along with effective ways to reduce or eliminate drinking problems such as underage drinking, drinking and driving, and binge drinking. The *In Their Own Words* section contains interviews with experts on a wide variety of alcohol-related issues, *In the News* provides current news articles for downloading, and *In My Opinion* offers essays including "It's Better to Teach Safe Use of Alcohol."

Drink Smart
website: www.drinksmart.org

Drink Smart is an electronic magazine, based in Canada, that believes encouraging responsible drinking by young people who have reached the legal age is a laudable goal. Drink Smart publishes personal stories on drinking and driving, the effects of alcohol on families, and attitudes towards drinking among teens and at colleges.

The Stanton Peele Addiction Website
website: www.peele.net

Stanton Peele has been researching and writing about addiction for thirty years. His controversial approach negates the American medical model of addiction as a disease. Instead, he views it as a behavior which can be overcome through maturity, improved coping skills, and better self-management and self-esteem. His website includes an "Ask Stanton" question and answer section and an extensive virtual library of articles available for viewing. Peele has also authored several books, including *The Truth About Addiction and Recovery* and *Diseasing of America*, which may be ordered from the website.

BIBLIOGRAPHY

Books

Henri Begleiter and Benjamin Kissin	*The Genetics of Alcoholism.* New York: Oxford University Press, 1995.
Christine Bichler	*Teen Drinking (Drug Abuse Prevention).* New York: Rosen Publishing, 2000.
Gayle M. Boyd, Jan Howard, and Robert A. Zucker, eds.	*Alcohol Problems Among Adolescents: Current Directions in Prevention Research.* Hillsdale, NJ: Lawrence Erlbaum, 1995.
Donald W. Goodwin	*Alcoholism: The Facts.* Oxford, Great Britain: Oxford University Press, 2000.
David J. Hanson	*Alcohol Education: What We Must Do.* Westport, CT: Praeger, 1996.
Raymond V. Haring	*Shattering Myths and Mysteries of Alcohol: Insights and Answers to Drinking, Smoking, and Drug Use.* Sacramento: Healthspan Communications, 1998.
Dwight B. Heath	*Drinking Occasions: Comparative Perspectives on Alcohol and Culture.* Philadelphia: Brunner/Mazel, 2000.
Harold D. Holder and Griffith Edwards, eds.	*Alcohol and Public Policy: Evidence and Issues.* Oxford: Oxford University Press, 1995.
Mark Gauvreau Judge	*Wasted: Tales of a Gen X Drunk.* Center City, MN: Hazelden Information Education, 1997.
Jean Kinney	*Loosening the Grip: A Handbook of Alcohol Information.* Boston: McGraw-Hill, 2000.
Ann Kirby-Payne	*Refuse to Use: A Girl's Guide to Drugs and Alcohol.* New York: Rosen Publishing, 1999.
John Langone	*Tough Choices: A Book About Substance Abuse.* Boston: Little, Brown and Co., 1995.
Hank Nuwer	*Wrongs of Passage: Fraternities, Sororities, Hazing, and Binge Drinking.* Bloomington: Indiana University Press, 1999.
Robert M. O'Neil	*Alcohol Advertising on the Air: Beyond the Reach of Government?* Washington, DC: The Media Institute, 1997.
Edmund B. O'Reilly	*Sobering Tales: Narratives of Alcoholism and Recovery.* Amherst: University of Massachusetts Press, 1997.
Stanton Peele	*The Diseasing of America: How We Allowed Recovery Zealots and the Treatment Industry to Convince Us We Are Out of Control.* San Francisco: Jossey-Bass, 1999.
Stanton Peele and Marcus Grant, eds.	*Alcohol and Pleasure: A Health Perspective.* Philadelphia: Brunner/Mazel, 1999.

Laurence P. Pringle   *Drinking: A Risky Business.* New York: Morrow
                               Junior Books, 1997.

Pam Richards   *Alcohol.* Chicago, IL: Heinemann Library, 2000.

Marc Alan Schuckit   *Educating Yourself About Alcohol and Drugs: A People's
                               Primer.* New York: Plenum Press, 1995.

Periodicals

Maria Luisa Alaniz   "Pro-Drinking Messages and Message Environments
and Chris Wilkes   for Young Adults: The Case of Alcohol Industry
                               Advertising in African American, Latino, and Native
                               American Communities," *Journal of Public Health
                               Policy,* vol. 19, no. 4, 1998. Available from 208
                               Meadowood Drive, South Burlington, VT 05403.

Shanta M. Bryant   "Poking a Hole in the Myths," *Christian Social Action,*
                               March 1999. Available from 100 Maryland Ave. NE,
                               Washington, DC 20002.

Shanta M. Bryant   "Youth Warning Other Youth About Drugs and
                               Alcohol," *Christian Social Action,* February 1998.

Adam Cohen   "Battle of the Binge," *Time,* September 8, 1997.

Larry Fritzlan   "Raising the Bottom," *Family Therapy Networker,*
                               July/August 1999. Available from 7705 13th St. NW,
                               Washington, DC 20012.

David M. Halbfinger   "Selling Alcohol Disguised as Punch," *The New York
                               Times,* July 27, 1997.

Dwight B. Heath   "Should We 'Just Say No' to Childhood Drinking?"
                               Priorities for Health, vol. 12, no. 2, 2000. Available
                               from 1995 Broadway, 2nd Floor, New York, NY 10023-
                               5860.

Jack Hitt   "The Battle of the Binge," *New York Times Magazine,*
                               October 24, 1999.

Constance Holden   "New Clues to Alcoholism Risk," *Science,* May 29,
                               1998.

Issues and Controversies   "Alcohol Issues," February 20, 1998. Available from
on File   Facts On File News Services, 11 Penn Plaza, New York,
                               NY 10001-2006.

Journal of the American   "Benefits and Dangers of Alcohol," January 6, 1999.
Medical Association   Available from PO Box 10945, Chicago, IL 60610.

John Leo   "Scotch the Ads? Absolut-ly!" *U.S. News & World
                               Report,* December 9, 1996.

David Leonhardt   "How Big Liquor Takes Aim at Teens," *Business Week,*
                               May 19, 1997.

Lance R. Odden   "Talk to Your Children About the Tough Stuff," *Vital
                               Speeches of the Day,* March 1, 1999.

Per Ola and   "I Can Quit Whenever I Want," *Reader's Digest,* June
Emily d'Aulaire   1997.

Patrick M. O'Malley,   "Alcohol Use Among Adolescents," *Alcohol Health &*
Lloyd D. Johnston,   *Research World*, vol. 22, no. 2, 1998. Available from
and Jerald G. Bachman   National Technical Information Service (NTIS), U.S.
                         Department of Commerce, 5285 Port Royal Rd.,
                         Springfield, VA 22161.

Stanton Peele   "Recovering from an All-or-Nothing Approach to
                         Alcohol," *Psychology Today*, September/October 1996.

Joyce Howard Price   "New Battle About Evil Spirits," *Insight on the News*,
                         February 1, 1999. Available from 3600 New York Ave.
                         NE, Washington, DC 20002.

Seth Schiesel   "On Web, New Threats Seen to the Young," *The New
                         York Times*, March 7, 1997.

Jacob Sullum   "Youth Appeal," *Reason*, June 1997.

J.J. Thompson   "Plugging the Kegs," *U.S. News & World Report*,
                         January 26, 1998.

USA Today   "Steering Kids Away from Problem Drinking,"
                         December 1998.

INDEX